Endorsements

Do you want to live a life that pleases the Lord and challenges others to go deeper, further, and higher? I have personally been impacted by the authentic spirit of faith in the life and ministry of Keith Miller. Now through *Surrender to the Spirit* you too can experience an impartation of the supernatural dimensions of God.

—JAMES W. GOLL
Cofounder, Encounters Network
Author, *The Seer*, *Dream Language*, and
The Lost Art of Intercession

Keith Miller's *Surrender to the Spirit* caused my heart to burn. It seemed that fire leapt from each page as I read his story and insights. We need more men like Keith, who love God with passion. And we need more books like this one—books that ignite people's hearts for God. I highly recommend it!

—BILL JOHNSON
Author, *When Heaven Invades Earth*

I fully endorse Keith Miller's book. By reading it, you will receive tremendous revelatory insights equipping you to better embrace the supernatural realm. These valid kingdom keys will help unlock the mystical mysteries that are being set before us. Truly we are in the mist of a spiritual revolution that will greatly affect how we define Christianity. Your faith will be increased and your understanding enlarged by applying the insights revealed in this book. Keith and Janet Miller are upright and awesome. Their lives and ministry are huge blessings to all who know them. Your spiritual life will be better equipped to advance deeper into the things of God by reading and applying the truths of this book.

—BOBBY CONNER
Founder, Eagles View Ministries
Demonstration of God's Power Ministries
www.bobbyconner.org

I know that Keith Miller is well acquainted with the wonderful, awesome person of the Holy Spirit. This relationship is very evident through the fruit of Keith's life and ministry. The keys of understanding that are contained in this book are true downloads from the Lord's presence—downloads that will change your life. These downloads come through a vessel who is well acquainted with the sevenfold Spirit of God!

—PATRICIA KING
Extreme Prophetic

As I read Keith Miller's book, I thought, *Is he hearing my very thoughts somehow?* I too have felt compelled in the last months to pray for the sevenfold Spirit of God to operate in my life. Not only is Keith an excellent writer—you should hear him speak! He's a "hoot," and you'll want to know what God is saying to him at any given minute. I love Keith's line, "Why don't you invite the Lord to demonstrate the Spirit of the Lord through your life, not in word only, but in a demonstration of the Spirit that will cause people to declare that 'surely God is with you.'" Preach it! Oh, and read it!

—STEVE SHULTZ
The Elijah List, www.elijahlist.com
Founder, *The Voice of the Prophetic* magazine

Surrender to the Spirit

Surrender to the Spirit

THE LIMITLESS POSSIBILITIES OF YIELDING TO THE HOLY SPIRIT

By

KEITH MILLER

Destiny Image® Publishers, Inc.
P.O. Box 310
Shippensburg, PA 17257-0310

"Speaking to the Purposes of God for this Generation
and for the Generations to Come."

For Worldwide Distribution, Printed in the U.S.A.

ISBN 10: 0-7684-2387-2

ISBN 13: 978-0-7684-2387-7

This book and all other Destiny Image, Revival Press, MercyPlace, Fresh Bread, Destiny Image Fiction, and Treasure House books are available at Christian bookstores and distributors worldwide.

For a U.S. bookstore nearest you, call
1-800-722-6774.

For more information on foreign distributors, call
717-532-3040.

Or reach us on the Internet:
www.destinyimage.com

2 3 4 5 6 7 8 9 10 11 / 09 08 07

Dedication

THIS book is dedicated to Father God, and how grateful I am to Him for His great love toward me. And wonderful Jesus, I can't put into words the depth of gratitude I have for You in my life. You are my life! Precious Holy Spirit, thank You so much for being with me everyday, teaching me, and releasing Your sevenfold function in and through my life for the glory of Jesus. Thank you, Father, Son, and Holy Spirit for Your fellowship and for revealing to me the deep things!

Contents

Acknowledgments

To my best friend, companion, and precious wife, Janet. Thank you for being you. You have always stood with me and encouraged me to go for it. I love you! What a great journey it is with you at my side.... Great days! Great things!

To my children; Keith, Lisa, Justin, Joshua, Alison , and Troy. You guys are the best. What a blessing the Lord has given me in you. It is awesome to see each of you grow strong in the Lord and your spiritual destiny in Him. I love you all very much!

To my precious grandsons, Ethan and Evan. You guys rock! And you keep Papa young! The Lord has already shown me so much about your coming days. Get ready....

To Pastor Benny and Suzanne Hinn. What a great blessing you both have been in our lives. We have learned so much about the ministry of the Holy Spirit being with you all

For all those who were willing to go where no one had gone before in the Lord. Thank you for being breakers for the many. Their breakthroughs are now our breakthroughs.

To my friends Todd and Shonna Bentley. Thank you, brother...you have been a great blessing to us.

To my friends Kevin and Shelly Prosch. Thank you for encouraging me and for the counsel of the Lord through you.

To my friends Bobby Conner, Bill Johnson, Paul Keith Davis, JoAnn McFatter, Patricia King, and Jill Austin, all of you have been great to minister with and an encouragement. Janet and I have great respect for each of you.

To my great staff at Stand Firm World Ministries. Thank you! What a great team! Thank You, Lord, for each and every one of them.

To those who help make sure the book was ready in time: Shae Cooke; Jackie Macgirvin; Patricia Gray; Laurie Johnson; Justin, Joshua, Troy and Janet Miller. The hours you spent on the editing and preparing was long and had to be done quickly. I am very grateful to each of you!

To Don Milam, thank you. I'm grateful to you for helping me and giving me the opportunity to publish the book.

To Destiny Image for all of your help in getting this book published. Thank you.

To all my wonderful partners. Thank you for standing with us.

To Jennifer Kingsley and Terrina Rieann for covering us in prayer.

Introduction

WE live in a day of crisis and yet opportunity. Shifting paradigms are all around us and they press into our world, they force us to do things differently and to see beyond what we and others have already seen. Even as I write this introduction, there's a deep stirring in my inner man as I sense the Holy Spirit's unction that every believer should walk, live, and operate out of the fullness of His precious presence, power, and purpose for our lives.

The Holy Spirit's desire is that you and I live every day in the fullness of the Lord, by seeing above and beyond what we can do, and that Jesus would receive glory and honor through His great power that works in us and through us. This is the essence of what Paul writes about in Ephesians 3:20-21: *"Now to Him who is able to do exceedingly abundantly above all that we ask or think, according to the power that works in us, to Him be glory in the church by Christ Jesus to all generations, forever and ever. Amen."*

Dear friends, I encourage you to believe that the Lord will release to you a revelation of the unlimited realm of the great ministry and fullness of the Holy Spirit in and through your life. Get ready! Ask right now, before we embark on this great journey together. Ask the Holy Spirit to open your spiritual eyes and ears to see the invisible, and to hear what He is saying to the Church in this season of history. Ask Him to open up the depths of the Word to His people and to reveal the secret things of the Kingdom—so that we can walk in a greater dimension of victory and thus be able to shift the course of history toward the fulfillment of God's ultimate purpose.

There are times during the course of human history where the Lord has revealed the secrets of the Kingdom to His church. These heavenly revelations released something specific that He had ordained for His people. Each time this occurred, something incredible happened. Martin Luther, the Jesus movement of the '60s, the Azusa Street revival, the Welsh revival—all were specific moves of God. These revelations by the Holy Spirit were poured out for that time and for that season. They had a great impact on the Church. I believe that the revelation of the function and flow of the sevenfold Holy Spirit in the believer's life is a revelation for today. It has the potential to release the Body of Christ into a greater depth of the Spirit-filled, Spirit-led life.

Praise the mighty name of Jesus, who pours out the promise of the Holy Spirit to us (see Acts 2:33)! Praise the mighty name of Jesus, who said, *"Peace to you! As the Father has sent Me, I also send you"* (John 20:21). The Father sent Jesus with an unlimited anointing of the Holy Spirit. (see John 3:34). That same promise is for us. The Lord is revealing, by His Spirit, a greater understanding of the seven Spirits of God that releases us into the sevenfold function of the Holy Spirit.

This spiritual dynamic that flows into us daily is the witness of the reality of the Holy Spirit's power to the masses of humanity. The unlimited anointing that the Lord is pouring out will reveal an even greater understanding of the ministry of the Holy Spirit. The Church will be plunged into the river that is widening the banks of spiritual realities and creating a tremendous overflow that will extend into the marketplaces of the world.

A few years ago, I had a profound prophetic encounter, which began a series of events that literally caused me to press in for deeper communion with the Lord. That encounter resulted in the release of the revelation that I am about to share with you on the "seven Spirits of God." This book is more than a few pages of awesome revelation—it's a commissioning of the Holy Spirit to see a people who walk and live in His fullness. Yes, Lord!

My prayer is that the most precious Holy Spirit would breathe upon His Word and cause it to become food for your hungry soul. I pray that you will be motivated in such a powerful way that it will lead you to a place of communion with the Father, which in turn will usher His fullness in and through your life. *Lord, let it be so, and let it be according to what You have made available to every believer at the Cross.*

CHAPTER 1

Life-Changing Visitation

SINCE I began my walk with the Lord in 1989, I have been blessed by tremendous prophetic encounters and visitations. In June 1994, during an increased time of holy desperation and yearning, I attended a Benny Hinn conference in Dallas, Texas, and received a powerful deposit of the anointing. This anointing radically changed my life. Over the next few years, the Lord moved mightily through my ministry in unbelievable ways—through healings, signs, wonders, and demonstrations of the Holy Spirit's power. I saw thousands impacted in many regions and nations.

Normal meetings became extended times of profound supernatural demonstrations of God's Word and power. Lives were completely transformed. Yet, even though God poured out so much upon my life and ministry, I knew deep in my spirit that there was something more, and I hungered for it.

In August 2002, in Amarillo, Texas, we were planning the school of revival. The Lord spoke to me that something powerful would happen. I pressed into God for something deeper. During one of the school sessions, the Lord gave me a life-changing prophetic vision that catapulted me to another level in Him.

Then in August during the worship at a meeting, I was caught up in the heavenlies and I saw a huge massive angel. He was the perfect picture of strength. He resonated with authority and might.

He shouted, "Open your mouth and eat this!" I did and he threw something into my mouth and I ate it! I thought, *what in the world was that?* It appeared to be a scroll or a book.

I had never experienced anything like it, even though prophetic encounters were not new to me. It blew me away. I grabbed my Bible, searched the Scriptures, and marked several passages that related to the experience. (See Ezekiel 3:1-4; Revelation 10:8-11.) My team, curious, asked me what had just happened. Although I was still in shock, I stammered, "I-I-just ate a scroll—the big angel threw it at me!" They looked just as surprised as I felt. This event launched a series of prophetic encounters with the Lord. For the next three months that experience had a profound impact on my ministry, my family, and in my life.

A SECOND ANGELIC ENCOUNTER

In September 2002, I had another encounter. I woke up one morning at 3 o'clock. I knew the Lord wanted to meet with me, so I got in my car and went to my office. Stepping inside, I felt the atmosphere in the room change instantly. The whole room was filled with the Lord's electrical presence, along with a deep holiness. It was as though the old atmosphere had been vacuumed out and a purity of the holiness of His presence came rushing in. I thought, *Yes, this is going to be one of those times.*

I kicked off my shoes and headed toward my office. At the back part of the corridor was the same massive angel who had given me the scroll. He radiated strength, power, and authority. I shook, I trembled, I came undone. I knew I was not having a vision. I was seeing him in the natural—he was as real as any human being. He looked down at me, unsmiling. I dashed right into my office and slammed the door. I said "Holy cow! OK, Lord, what's going on?" And I began to pray.

My heart was racing. My desire was to seek God's purpose. I cried out to be a vessel, a proclaimer to release the heart and mind of the Father. During this time, the Lord pulled down a heavenly movie screen. He showed me the counsel of His heart and strategies for citics and regions. I got all excited. After about 45 minutes of divine instruction I knew the Holy Spirit was finished talking to me.

I said, "OK, Holy Spirit, what's up with the big angel in the hall?"

He said, "Go look; he's got a name on each arm."

I had to muster up some courage to see if he was still there. I was sure all the cloud of witnesses in Heaven were laughing at me. But you must understand—this guy was huge! I looked, and sure enough; he was still there. There was a name on each arm.

Stature and strength!

Then he was gone. The Lord spoke to me that the Body of Christ needs stature and strength to begin walking in the next level of the commissioning and deposit of the anointing He wants to release to us. To walk in those realms, we can't be weak. We have to be people strengthened in our inner man, so as to completely fulfill and be finishers of *that which is given* us to do. We have to walk in the maturity of Christ in us.

Right now, you may be in a place of character and strength building. Embrace that. As the Holy Spirit reveals His depth to us, the mature stature of Christ forms in us. A new level of destiny requires us to ask the Lord to "Search me, and try me!" It demands that we walk not by our ability, but by that very character and stature of Christ in us as mature sons and daughters in the Lord.

The angel actually had a name on each leg as well, but I haven't been released to share those yet.

A THIRD MEETING AND A
THRONE ROOM ENCOUNTER

After that experience in September, I was invited to preach at seven days of meetings. During preparation, I spent time down on the floor of the pastor's office. I asked the Lord for the counsel of Heaven for the meetings, the church, and the region. Instantly I was caught up before the Lord's throne. It was massive, full of energy, majestic, filled with glory, and white. It was an incredible experience to see the Lord. Power! Glory! I do not have the words to adequately describe the magnitude of power that radiated from Him. It was just so intense. It took my breath away—literally.

The same angel was there again, and I saw the Lord pass an envelope to him. Then the angel came to me and handed me the envelope. Now I was totally blown away. I took the envelope but was in such awe that I dropped it. The angel picked it up and handed it back. You have got to understand that I was totally flipping out the whole time. I opened the envelope. Inside were written two Scriptures: Revelation 4: 5 and. Isaiah 11:2

> *And from the throne proceeded lightnings, thunderings, and voices. Seven lamps of fire were burning before the throne, which are the seven Spirits of God* (Revelation 4:5).

> *The Spirit of the Lord shall rest upon Him, the Spirit of wisdom and understanding, the Spirit of counsel and might, the Spirit of knowledge and of the fear of the Lord* (Isaiah 11:2).

Since this encounter, I have been on an intense journey with the Lord to learn about the Seven Fold Spirit of God, which are the seven manifestations of the one Holy Spirit. I now teach and minister out of a deep flow of this revelation, which many Christians have never heard of. The last few years have been a time of awesome spiritual growth.

THE CALL

God showed me that He is calling His people to a new level—a place where these seven Spirits of God are activated and flowing within each of our lives through deep communion with the Holy Spirit. Why does He call? Why does He desire this deep, intimate communion with us? Because He wants to reveal more of Himself to His children. That's you and me! He longs for us to enter into a deeper level of holy pursuit and holy hunger. It's a stirring of the Holy Spirit so deep within that it awakens our inner man, so that *we know, that we know, that we know* there is something more He desires to share with us. We ache, thirst, hunger, and yearn for it. The only thing that will satiate, fill, and satisfy is deep intimacy and communion with Him.

Blaise Pascal, the French philosopher, said that all mankind was created with a vacuum that can only be filled with God. God has sent His sevenfold Spirit to fill that empty place in our lives.

When we commune with God, the Holy Spirit searches out the deep counsel of God and reveals it to us: *"But God has revealed them to us through His Spirit. For the Spirit searches all things, yes, the deep things of God"* (1 Cor. 2:10).

How do we stimulate the thirst, fuel the hunger, and kindle the yearning? The Word tells us that the Holy Spirit stirs it up! *"Call to Me, and I will answer you, and show you great and mighty things, which you do not know"* (Jer. 33:3). The Hebrew word *mighty*, in the context of Jeremiah 33:3, means "inaccessible." God wants to release something to us that was once inaccessible; He wants to reveal to us the deep counsel of God that Deuteronomy 29:29 tells us *"belong to us and to our children forever."*

GOD OPENS THE DOOR

In Revelation 3:20, there is a great invitation from the Lord to the Church: *"Behold, I stand at the door and knock. If anyone hears My voice and opens the door, I will come in to him and dine with him, and he with Me."* This refers to visitation or communion of a greater degree. The power of your "yes" will cause something wonderful and glorious to take place. What is it? It's found a few verses later in Revelation 4:1. We see now an invitation to go through the door that is opened by the Lord: *"After these things I looked, and behold, a door standing open in heaven. And the first voice which I heard was like a trumpet speaking with me, saying, 'Come up here, and I will show you things which must take place after this.'"* He is the door or gate that ascends to a place where we will meet Him. Every prophetic encounter that I have at this level has been a life-changing time for me—a true encounter with the Lord.

THE SEVEN SPIRITS OF GOD

Revelation 3:1 describes Jesus as *"He who has the seven Spirits of God and the seven stars."* From John 3:34 we learn that Jesus has the anointing without measure: *"For He [Jesus] is sent by God. He speaks God's words, for God's Spirit is upon Him with out measure or limit"* (NLT). We find the seven Spirits of God listed in Isaiah 11:2. Each of these great flows of the precious Holy Spirit is available to every believer. God desires us to see every function and expression of the sevenfold Spirit of God in and through our lives.

Paul declared that his "*speech and...preaching were not with persuasive words of human wisdom, but in demonstration of the Spirit and of power*" (1 Cor. 2:4). Notice he said the Spirit and power. The Lord wants to release in and through your life rivers of living water so that your life would daily demonstrate the Holy Spirit's flow.

> *On the last day, that great day of the feast, Jesus stood and cried out, saying, "If anyone thirsts let him come to Me and drink. He who believes in Me, as the Scripture has said, out of his heart will flow rivers of living water." But this He spoke concerning the Spirit, whom those believing in Him would receive; for the Holy Spirit was not yet given, because Jesus was not yet glorified* (John 7.37-39).

Here the Lord shared that out of our hearts shall flow rivers of living water. "Rivers" (plural) is indicating multiple, continuous flows of the precious Holy Spirit day after day, without limit. There is only one Holy Spirit—but seven functions or expressions of the Holy Spirit as described in Isaiah 11:2 and Revelation 4:5.

The first flow of the sevenfold expression of the Holy Spirit is the *Spirit of the Lord upon*, or God's manifest presence. This means communion with the Lord and a place of intimacy with Him that in turn releases the rest of the expressions in and through our lives. We must begin with an encounter with God's manifest presence, and then all seven functions flow out of His presence: wisdom, understanding, counsel, might, knowledge, and the fear of the Lord.

ABIDING IN HIM

We must abide in Jesus and His presence to operate fully in the seven functions of the Holy Spirit. Everything flows out of the anointing—out of the branch. That branch is Jesus: "*There shall come forth a Rod from the stem of Jesse, and a Branch shall grow out of his roots*" (Isa. 11:1). Everything flows out of Christ. We cannot operate in the sevenfold anointing without first being in the branch.

> *I am the vine, you are the branches. He who abides in Me, and I in him, bears much fruit; for without Me you can do nothing* (John 15:5).

> *And if some of the branches were broken off, and you, being a wild olive tree, were grafted in among them, and with them became a partaker of the root and fatness of the olive tree* (Romans 11:17).

If you seek God, He will equip you to operate in the fullness of His holy presence. The rivers will be loosed in you, toward you, for you, and through you. In intimacy and communion, the Lord will reveal the *sevenfold operation* of the Holy Spirit. He will uncap the rivers of His manifest presence: the Spirit of wisdom and understanding, the Spirit of counsel and might, the Spirit of knowledge and of the fear of the Lord. He will allow you to experience a new dimension of communion with Him for a new outpouring of His presence.

By His divine power, we will be partakers of His nature in us. Press into that place of intimacy with Him, that place of abiding in His presence and anointing so He is free to release all seven functions of His Spirit in your life. Through His grace, God will pour this sevenfold blessing out upon you.

My prayer for you is that the Holy Spirit will introduce Himself to you beyond any dimension you have ever known. How much you embrace Him, press into Him, and commune with Him is going to determine His increase in your life. Pray and ask the Holy Spirit for a true friendship—a length, width, depth, and height of communion together greater than you have ever known. Then the deep things of God will be revealed. It is our blessing and privilege as His children to know the mysteries, secrets, and thoughts of God. I'm convinced that every believer has a potential to operate out of this fullness. It is our inheritance. (See Romans 8:16.) Isn't that spectacular? The Lord Himself is our great inheritance.

We are called not just to operate in an occasional gift, but also to live in a place of perpetual flow of the Holy Spirit. As a believer, you can wake up every day in fresh anointing; you can live as an overcomer. You can be a finisher of the race that God has called you to run. You can do exceedingly abundantly above and beyond anything you can think or imagine, according to God's power that works for you and from you. Every believer has the potential to see the impossible become possible. I long for you to know Him, not just as "holy," but also "wholly," with every fiber of your being filled with Him, moment by moment, for now and evermore.

Every blessing is ours in the heavenly realms, and we are seated in those heavenly places by one spirit with the Lord (see Eph. 2:6). In the following chapters, we'll examine the seven Spirits of God in more detail and learn how to activate them so that they flow within our lives. Deep to deep—as you engage in those deep things of God, they will wreck you and forever change you, because you will know the deep, deep, deep, places in Him. *"Deep calls unto deep at the noise of Your waterfalls; all Your waves and billows have gone over me"* (Ps. 42:7).

Holy Spirit, You are the Spirit of Truth. You will teach us the deep things of God. Thank You for teaching all that there is to know about the Lord. I'm hungry after the deep things of God. In Jesus' mighty Name, Amen!

CHAPTER 2

Encountering the Holy Spirit

W HEN God's manifest presence enters a room, His presence alone transforms you. There is incredible passion, insatiable hunger, and a desire to go deep-to-deep in Him. He grips you to reveal the depth of His love in enormous ways.

The revelation I received of Him in those encounters in the early days sparked an almost uncontainable fervor and zeal in me. I was so on fire for the Lord, that one day I asked my pastor to "loan" me a number of people from the church. I wanted them to go with me to win Miami, Texas, for God!

"I need that person, and that one…oh, and the worship leader, too," I said eagerly.

"Keith, hold on," he replied.

But nothing could quench the fire in my bones. I wanted to tell the world about God.

However, I still spent hours and hours in prayer, at His feet yearning to go deeper, craving His presence. I knew God had more for me, and I wanted to ascend those new levels—those new realms of my destiny in Him. God did have more for me, as I was to find out in a series of perfectly orchestrated events, over the next few years. There was a powerful, awesome anointing, and a deeper revelation of the Holy Spirit yet to come.

These powerful visitations from the Lord have literally changed my life. When I was a Southern Baptist youth pastor at our home church in a small Texas town, one of the deacons' wives approached me one day and handed me a videotape.

"Take this. Put it in your coat. Watch it, because this guy reminds us of you," she said.

I walked out with the tape bulging in my coat pocket like I was stealing something. I wondered what in the world she had given me. When I got home, my wife, Janet, and I sat down, excited to watch the video. We turned it on, and this poofy-haired guy came on the screen. He took his coat off and threw it on people, and the people started falling down.

I said "Whoa!" But what I saw did not offend me.

And then he said, "Take the anointing!" All the people in the chairs started falling out everywhere. But that did not offend me, either. But then a lady walked up onto the platform, and this guy looked at her and said, "You want this anointing, baby?"

Now that offended me! My wife and I just looked at each other in amazement. All I could think of was, *That can't be God!*

"God doesn't talk like that!" I said to my wife. "There's no *way* God could talk like that."

Click! I turned off the video. I wondered what the deacon's wife saw in this man that reminded her of me. Just as quickly as she had thrust that tape at me, I thrust it out of my mind.

In 1994, I was the senior pastor of a church. I'll never forget one Sunday morning I was sitting at my desk trying to get a message together. I felt broken and frustrated. I had no idea what to preach about anymore because people still left the church broken and crying. There was little change in their lives. My heart really hurt for them—something was missing. I knew there had to be more. But what?

I bowed my head and prayed, "What's missing, Lord?"

Something incredible happened. I started remembering the glory of those early encounters. I remembered the visitations. I remembered the days in 1990 and 1991 that I spent hours and hours in prayer and deep communion with the Lord. I started remembering the times my whole office was literally filled with the Lord's manifest presence, and the morning when I had such a powerful encounter with the Lord that I became truly aware of His vastness, of how awesome and glorious He really is. I will never forget that morning. God revealed such a depth of Himself that I could say from then on, with great confidence, "Oh Lord God, You made the heavens and the earth and there is nothing impossible for You!"

For two years I had had such powerful encounters with the Lord. But this morning in 1994, the Holy Spirit started stirring my inner man, reminding me of those deep times. He started releasing a great hunger deep within me. I had forgotten His presence.

At that moment I remembered the statement that I had made many times. If you can look back and see a time that you were more passionate for the Lord than you are now, that means you are backslidden. Right at that moment I closed my Bible and said, "O Lord, I want those days again. I don't care if I ever preach again; don't care if I ever minister again; the only thing I want is your Holy presence!"

Now understand this, what I offered to the Lord was something that had a profound significance and importance in my life. This was not just a religious cliché. I loved to preach. I loved to minister. I gave up my success in the business world. It was my deepest passion to preach and minister for the Lord. It was like fire in my bones. So when I said I would give up preaching, it was no small gesture! The only thing I wanted was the Lord's presence. I was like Moses on the mountain when he declared in Exodus 33:12-14:

*See, You say to me, "Bring up this people." But You
have not let me know whom You will send with me. Yet
You have said, "I know you by name, and you have also
found grace in My sight." Now therefore, I pray, if I have
found grace in Your sight, show me now Your way, that
I may know You and that I may find grace in Your
sight. And consider that this nation is Your people." And
He said, "My Presence will go with you, and I will give
you rest."*

I read that. If I find grace in His sight, He knows me by name,
and His presence will go with me, and He will give me rest. This
is what *rest* means: God's presence will give rest to His people.
That is, His presence soothes, comforts, settles, consoles, and qui-
ets us, but it also means the resting of the Spirit of God upon.

"Oh, Lord, I need Your rest. I'm asking for You, right here in my
office. If I find grace in Your sight—and I know I have grace,
because Jesus says He gives me grace—I'm asking just like
Moses. I'm asking for Your presence to come upon me right now.
I want Your glory. I want Your glory to come and rest upon me. I
don't care if I ever preach or minister again, but there is one
thing I've got to have. It's Your holy presence upon me. I'm asking for You to come and rest upon me."

Right at that moment, my whole office once again filled with
the Lord's holy presence, and the rest of God came upon me and
settled upon me and did not leave for days and days and days!
This experience, this time of holy desperation, launched me into
a series of events that released me into the anointing that I
believe we are walking in right now.

For the next four months, I was up every morning at 5:30
seeking God. Psalm 63 became my daily cry: "Oh God, I long to
see Your power and Your glory in the sanctuary." I read it, prayed

it, and cried it out every morning at 5:30. I never missed a morning. It ached so deeply within me.

This happened in March of 1994, but I'll never forget what happened about a month later when I read Acts 1:8: *"But you shall receive power when the Holy Spirit has come upon you...."* I had read Acts 1:8 before; I had preached Acts 1:8 many times from the pulpit. I knew that the word "power" there means *dunamis* power, which is "miracle working ability." But I had to be honest with myself—I wasn't seeing the miraculous, the miracle working ability, even though I preached it.

That was soon to change.

One morning at 5:30, I turned on the television and was going through the channels, and guess who I saw? That same poofy-haired guy from the video I had watched five years before.

I said, "I am not going to watch that guy!" and kept flipping through the channels. I went right through all the channels and came right back to him. All of a sudden, a young boy who was on the platform with the preacher started yelling.

"Yeah, God just healed me! I couldn't run, and all the kids at school made fun of me, but look what God did!" and he went running across the platform. The camera showed his parents crying. It showed the little boy crying. It showed the evangelist crying.

If the camera had panned to me, it would have recorded me on the floor of my front room, crying, and longing for the power of God to manifest in my ministry in the same way it did right there in that service.

I cried out, "O Lord! I want Your power and glory in Your sanctuary!"

At that moment, Benny Hinn (the evangelist with the hair) looked directly into the camera and said, "There's a preacher, and you're in your front room crying, and you're saying that you want this anointing, and the Lord says, 'You can have it!'"

God got my attention as I lay there crying on the front room floor. Yes, this was the same guy who had totally offended me five years before. But here I was on my front room floor, crying out to the Lord for His power and glory—and now I had seen this young boy instantly healed.

I longed for that type of anointing. So every morning at 5:30 I watched him—Benny Hinn. I didn't tell my wife for a month. One day she was doing dishes, and I came up beside her and started drying them. She immediately knew something was going on because I don't do dishes! She asked me what was up.

I decided to be forthright and said, "Well…ah…what do you think about this Benny Hinn guy?"

"Why?"

"Well, I've kind of been watching him every morning at 5:30…"

My wife said, "I've been watching him every day at 1:30!"

"Really!" I said. That really blew me away. "What did you think?"

"I like it," she replied. Then she told me that they were having a Holy Spirit conference in Dallas. "I think we should go."

"We can't do that—we've got a reputation!"

"We could go," she said. "They wouldn't even know. We could just say we were attending a conference, but not say whose. Then they would release us to go."

I said, "Yeah, but it's for partners of the ministry only. We're not partners; there's no way we can get in. It's probably out of the question."

Her answer was, "All you have to do is call, and we'll use this as a sign: if they say we can come, then we're supposed to go."

When I called I actually talked to the main overseer of the entire partners' organization, and I told her, "Hi, my name is Keith Miller. I'm a Southern Baptist preacher. My wife and I have been watching your show, and we really like it. We would like to come to the conference in Dallas, but we thought since we aren't partners we probably can't come."

I was really trying to talk her out of it, but she said, "You know, I really believe that you're supposed to be here. We'll waive the partnership thing. The conference is already full, but when you get here ask for me, and I'm going to get you in. You just come on down to Dallas."

I said, "Oh!"

Then I asked my wife, "What about our reputation?"

She answered, "I know, but it looks like we're on our way to Dallas."

The church had offered to send us to any conference we wanted. So I told them I would like to take a few days off and go to a conference, but I didn't say whose. They told me to get the plane tickets and the room. The only catch—they didn't know it was Benny Hinn.

We arrived in Dallas, got off the plane, and even then I said to my wife, "Maybe we should pray about this."

She answered, "We're going."

When we arrived at the conference, my jaw dropped. There had to be at least 3,000 people lined up at the five doors waiting to get in. I was amazed there were that many people standing outside eager to go to a church service! I had never seen that.

When we got inside, they sat us in the third row from the front. I was ready, I had my Bible open. Countless thoughts flew through my mind and battled with my heart.

"I'm going to watch everything this guy says," I told my wife. "And the first time he makes one little mistake, I am out of here."

Within moments of Benny's arrival, Janet and I became glued to our chairs.

"There's a healing flow of the Holy Spirit right now," Benny said.

I barely had time to say, "Where?"

The healing anointing pervaded the very atmosphere of the room. The impossible and the unbelievable happened all around us. There was one woman in a wheelchair that they pushed down to the platform—and before I knew it, she walked past me pushing her own wheelchair back up the aisle!

She looked right at me and said, "What do you think about this?"

I just said, "Wow!" I saw this myself; with my own eyes I saw the whole thing! I could not believe what I had just seen!

I had told Janet, "There is no way that I'm going to go up there. I know he calls for preachers, but there is *no way* I'm going up there." But I had just seen God miraculously heal the woman in the wheelchair.

Then the inevitable happened. My heart was beating fast as Benny said, "All you preachers who want this anointing, get up here right now."

Without hesitation, without even a moment's thought, and without batting an eyelid, I leapt out of my chair and made my way to the platform. I was so desperate and so hungry for the anointing that I even forgot my manners. My mom had taught me to be polite, but I found myself literally pushing people out of my way. In my mind I was saying, *You aren't a preacher—move!* Even so, the whole time I was asking myself, *What are you doing?* And the answer was, *I don't know!* But my heart was say-ing, *hungry*. So I listened to my heart.

When I reached the platform I had no idea what to expect. Benny was on the other side of the platform. He turned around and looked at me, his expression almost fiery hot. He looked mad, and for a minute I thought maybe he had heard my inner battle and was coming at me in anger. With a fiery look he said, "Take the anointing!"

The next thing I knew I was falling down, and two huge guys picked me up by my belt and escorted me off the platform! You can imagine what that looked like. So much for reputation.

As soon as I got back to my seat, Janet wanted to know, "What was it like?"

I said, "I don't know. I went *poof*, and then they picked me up. I don't know!"

We go back to the hotel, and my wife asked again, "Come on, come on, tell me! What was it like?"

I said, "I really don't know! I'm not kidding, it just went *boom* when he looked at me, then *bam* I'm back up; and the next thing I know, I'm trying to walk. But I liked it!"

For the majority of the conference we were in the second row. The last night, we were caught in the crowd at the door and pushed out of the way, so we ended up sitting in the very back.

I told the Lord, "That's OK, Lord. I've enjoyed the front seats for three days; I don't mind sitting back here."

All of a sudden, Benny began ministering in the anointing, and he jumped off the platform, and was picking people out, moving through the crowd. I was just watching, thinking to myself, *Yeah, come on, I want it!* People were lying out all over the floor and I kept saying to myself *Wow!* Then he turned around and went back up to the platform. I told the Lord, "No, no, no, no, Lord! I came here for an impartation—I'm not looking at Benny Hinn, but I want that anointing that he has! Now Lord, I know that You witnessed to my inner man that this is You. I believe this is a holy invitation by the Holy Spirit so I can have this same anointing, because You revealed it to me. I want that anointing!"

Suddenly Benny turned back around, and just as though he had holy radar, he started heading back toward us.

I was thinking, *Yeah, come on back here!* (I didn't know this until later, but my wife, who had been so adamant about our attending in the first place, was secretly saying to herself, *Please don't let him come over here!*)

Benny shouted, "Those two!" Next thing I knew, Janet and I were being jerked right out to the aisle! I was saying *Yeah!*

Benny said, "You want this anointing—take this anointing!"

Then *boom!* I was on the floor under the anointing. I woke up about 15 minutes later and looked at my beautiful, elegant wife lying there on the floor beside me.

"I don't know how long we're supposed to stay on the floor," I said. "But I think we'd better try to get back to our seats."

My wife crawled to her chair, tried to sit down in her stylish dress, started laughing, and fell right back out of her seat. I stood up and began to worship the Lord. I distinctly felt somebody touch the back of my neck, but when I turned around, nobody was there. All of sudden I felt like someone took a bucket of oil and poured it out on me—it went all over me. At that moment, I knew I had received the anointing. I just remember thinking, *Oh, yeah! This is good.*

Our first Sunday back in our church, the Holy Spirit said, "Appropriate that which has been given." In a Baptist church? So I hid the anointing oil behind the plants on the pulpit. I read all the Scriptures in Acts about oil and the Holy Spirit, and I read James 5:14, "*Is anyone among you sick? Let him call for the elders of the church, and let them pray over him, anointing him with oil in the name of the Lord."*

Then I said, "And we just happen to have some oil here today. How many are sick?"

The first one up was Justin, my son. He had been hit in the eye by a crabapple and was told he'd lost so much of his sight that his eye would always be blurring from that point on. So I took the oil and anointed him and prayed.

Down he went. He actually crumbled to the floor. I couldn't believe it! It worked! And he was completely healed! All of sudden I had the church's attention. The front began filling up fast!

I couldn't believe all the sick people in my church. They just kept coming, and I prayed, and they were falling down. I started having fun! Then my mom, who is a conservative Baptist, came to the front.

I asked her, "Mom, are you sick?"

She said, "No, I just want that."

When I anointed her—I swear to you as the Lord is my witness—fire shot out of the end of my finger. It hit her right in the middle of her head. It hit her, hit the man who was trying to catch for me; together they hit the first pew, which hit the second pew and they all landed in the third!

I yelled, "Now that's *power*!"

I never wanted to copy Benny Hinn, but I believed I received an impartation of the anointing. Yes, that was power imparted to me from the Lord through Benny Hinn on the platform! The very same person who had offended my mind was instrumental in my stepping into my destiny. Many times I had open visions of meetings where thousands of people were being healed and changed. I could have allowed my stinking thinking to rob me of what the

Lord's heart was for me. The Lord wants our minds renewed so we can receive all that He has for us.

*L*ord, *I pray for every person reading this right now—that they would receive from You to them a mighty anointing of the Holy Spirit. Amen!*

CHAPTER 3

The Treasure of the Anointing

WE need divine impartation of the anointing. This can come in many different ways and different settings. It happened for me at a Benny Hinn service. There was an instant and brand-new release of the Lord's presence and power that has impacted my daily life and ministry ever since.

I wasn't interested in taking on Benny's personality or in trying to be him. I just wanted the impartation of the anointing on his ministry, while allowing the personality of the Holy Spirit to flow through me.

Elisha is a biblical example of this principle. He followed Elijah's ministry for years, and God spoke to his heart that he would receive the same mantle that was on Elijah's life. Because the Lord spoke this, he knew, he knew, he knew. Nobody could talk him out of waiting for that mantle. And they tried! Finally, after years of following Elijah, Elisha received the mantle. There was no doubt in his mind, and even his critics had to admit that they saw the spirit of Elijah on him. God not only gave Elisha the anointing, but He gave him a double portion. Even so, Elisha never took on Elijah's personality. (See Second Kings 2:1-10.)

GOD WILL EQUIP YOU

Each and every one of you has a vision or a dream to live out. But God doesn't expect you to do it in your ability. God wants to equip you with the exact anointing needed to carry out those dreams. He wants to give you an impartation from the Father so you walk in the anointing He's destined for your life. Even if He gives you that anointing through impartation, you still keep your own uniqueness. Ask God for the anointing! It isn't reserved for a select few. It's for you, it's for me, and it's for every believer. It can happen at any time, in a second, in a moment, even as you read these pages.

IMPARTING SPIRITUAL GIFTS

Paul expounds on revelation he received from Jesus in the following passage:

> *But I make known to you, brethren, that the gospel which was preached to me is not according to man. For I neither received it from man, nor was I taught it, but it came through the revelation of Jesus Christ. ...to reveal His Son in me, that I might preach Him among the Gentiles, I did not immediately confer with flesh and blood* (Galatians 1:11-12,16).

Jesus made the Gospel known to Paul. Everything Paul was walking and ministering in came from the revelation of Jesus. He did not confer with flesh and blood. Jesus released impartation to him.

Paul truly understood impartation, and he couldn't wait for God to impart His anointing on those to whom he ministered, so they could fully walk in the potential of their identity in the Lord. Paul ministered out of a great realm of revelation and anointing. Impartation is an infusing. Not just *on*, but *in*. He says, "The impartation is going to be spiritual. It doesn't come from me. I'm just going to be a vessel, a signpost. When I lay hands on you, because of the times I've met with Jesus and received impartation, I know what's going to happen. When you receive this, it's going to help you in what God has for your life."

God wants you to understand that the same anointing is available to every believer and it is priceless, precious, and to your advantage. In Paul's Epistle to the Romans he writes, "*For I long to see you, that I may impart to you some spiritual gift, so that you may be established*" (Rom. 1:11).

Paul knew the Holy Spirit wanted to release spiritual impartation upon those Roman Christians that would keep them steadfast in their purpose. The word *establish* is important. It means "to set fast, to turn resolutely in a certain direction." When God establishes His people through the impartation of His anointing, it's not only to touch them, but to sustain them in their destiny.

Fueling the depth of this Scripture is a passion of the Holy Spirit that Paul brings out so beautifully. Paul writes, "I long to see you!" He uses strong words of compassion here. The wording actually means "my heart is aching to see you."

I can completely relate to that statement. After living on the road for 12 or 14 days, all I want to do is go home and see my family. My heart pulsates as I anticipate our reunion. I talk with Janet sometimes 10 or 12 times a day while on the road, but it's not the same as being with her. Only seeing her satisfies that longing in my soul.

The Holy Spirit knows what was determined for you before the foundation of the world. He knows exactly what your purpose is. And He desperately wants to impart the anointing upon you to fulfill that purpose.

> *But as it is written: "Eye has not seen, nor eye heard, nor have entered into the heart of man the things which God has prepared for those who love **Him**." But God has revealed them to us through His Spirit. For the Spirit searches all things, yes, the deep things of God* (1 Corinthians 2:9-10).

Just as Paul longed to release spiritual gifts to his followers, the Holy Spirit can't wait to release a gift to *you*. Tell the Lord that you can't wait to receive it, either! Right now, right where you are, you can receive this gift from the Holy Spirit. Ask Him to release a divine impartation for your destiny. Declare this: "Holy Spirit, You know my future. According to John 16:14-15, the Word says You will transmit to me what Jesus is declaring about me. I know the Lord knew me before the foundations of the earth. I know He knew me before I was ever born. And right now I ask You for a divine impartation of the anointing, which will equip me for what You intend for my life."

DON'T SQUANDER THE ANOINTING

I believe there is a holy shift in the Church today. We will begin to cherish the things we once took lightly, because God is going to bring a new level of understanding and revelation about them. To *cherish* means "to treasure, adore, value." We must say, "Holy Spirit, I cherish impartation." Because impartation, according to the word *establish* in the Greek, is what resolutely keeps us going in the right direction.

God is calling us to new levels. I believe that it's going to be more than just touch, fall down, get up, and see you later.

True riches are His holy presence and anointing. Those who are wise value the oil of His presence and do not squander it. With His anointing the impossible becomes possible for every believer.

At a set of meetings a couple of years ago, I asked, "Lord, increase Your anointing."

He said, "You've got to understand, Keith, the beauty of impartation."

Proverbs 21:20 is one of the Scriptures He gave me. What a powerful passage! "*There is desirable treasure, and oil in the dwelling of the wise, but a foolish man squanders it.*" This refers to the wealth of His holy presence—the greatest deposit of all deposits, the greatest treasure of all treasures. That word *desirable* means "delight." The word *treasure* means "deposit." Oil always represents the Holy Spirit. It is the most beautiful thing to desire this deposit of His oil, of His anointing on your life, and to cherish it. We should learn to cherish His presence. We can't do that by our own efforts, but by the revelation of the Holy Spirit.

Here's a key to cherishing this anointing: intimacy with the Lord. (See John 15:5.) The vine feeds the branch. When you're hooked into the vine, you're hooked into the flow. Ask the Lord to increase that level of intimacy with Him in your life. Say this, like Paul and like Moses, "I want to become progressively, deeply, and intimately acquainted with You."

JESUS IMPARTS TO THE TWELVE

Mark 3:14-15 says that Jesus "*appointed twelve, that they might be with Him and that He might send them out to preach, and to have power to heal sickness and to cast out demons.*" Luke 9:1 says, "*Then He called His twelve disciples together and gave them power and authority over all demons, and to cure diseases.*" He gave it to them. They took the impartation and they healed the sick and ministered to everyone they met.

John 20:21-22 says, "*So Jesus said to them again, 'Peace to you! As the Father has sent Me, I also send you.' And when He had said this, He breathed on them, and said to them, 'Receive the Holy Spirit.'*" God sent Jesus out with an immeasurable anointing of the Holy Spirit. Jesus told the disciples He was going to send them out like His Father had sent Him. That means Jesus imparted an immeasurable anointing to them, too.

WE ARE HIS WORKMANSHIP

Every believer has received a measure of impartation and anointing, but God wants to increase more in you. Because you're His temple and His workmanship, He wants to manifest His glory, His nature, His character, and His power through your life. It still blows my mind that He chose to do it like that! Remember this Scripture? "*But we have this treasure in earthen vessels, that the excellence of the power may be of God and not of us*" (2 Cor. 4:7).

God's a builder. And the building He is doing is taking place in you. God wants an eternal impartation from the Holy Spirit to you because He knows your future. He has already written your book. He knows exactly what you need and when you need it, and He wants to release it to you.

Jesus, being a wise Master Builder, is not going to cut corners. He's going to do it all, step by step, line by line, and precept by precept. Why? Ephesians 2:10a says, "*We are His workmanship.*" He's doing a work in you and has ordained good works for you— but it's never by your might, never by your ability and never by your power. It is only by the power of the Holy Spirit. Do you want impartation like that from the Lord? God wants to give you a download for your life—an impartation of new levels, new mantles, a new anointing, and a new commission! Not from a man, not a natural blessing, but from the Lord. Ask the Lord for a divine life-changing and life-establishing impartation especially for you! Ask Him, and then by faith receive!

ASK FOR DIVINE IMPARTATION

God's Word says, "*Ask, and it will be given to you*" (Matt 7:7a). Have you been asking? If so, you will receive impartation of the Word of God that will burn like fire in your bones! If you want this, align yourself and say, "I'm hungry. I'm so hungry for You, Lord Jesus."

That is how it happened for me. I asked, I sought, and I knocked. I was so hungry for the Lord. Do you want to see God's power and His glory, today? It's not just for past saints; it's for you, us, today. Many are crying out as King David did while in the wilderness of Judea:

> *O God, You are my God; early will I seek You; my soul thirsts for You; my flesh longs for You in a dry and thirsty land where there is no water. So I have looked for You in the sanctuary, to see Your power and Your glory* (Psalm 63:1-2).

This Scripture became my cry!

I believe there is a generation right now who is crying out the same Scripture. "We want to see Your power and Your glory! We don't want to just hear of what You used to do. We have heard and read of some of the great things You have done throughout history and we are grateful. But we ask now for a Holy Spirit download of impartation from You so we may see those things you have purposed for our generation. We want today's manna."

I believe that is why you are reading this right now. You have a holy hunger that can't be satisfied by the natural. It can only be filled by the Holy Spirit and His mighty flow for your life. Ask right now for a mighty outpouring, a divine impartation from Him to you.

Use David's desert cry for your model: "*My soul shall be satisfied as with marrow and fatness, and my mouth shall praise You with joyful lips*" (Ps. 63:5). Ask God to pour out a mighty anointing upon you—to release the rich, abundant anointing of the Holy Spirit. Ask Him to saturate you with such rich anointing that you can't help but be joyful, can't help but speak of His lovingkindness. We need the perpetual, unlimited flow of the Holy Spirit's oil and, we need it every day. Let Psalm 92:10 be released right now! "*But my horn You have exalted like a wild ox; I have been anointed with fresh oil.*"

The world needs to see a people who are not walking in the power of man or what religion can give, but from the power of the precious Holy Spirit. "*And my speech and preaching were not with persuasive words of human wisdom, but in demonstration of the Spirit and of power, that your faith should not be in the wisdom of men but in the power of God*" (1 Cor. 2:4-5).

I remember reading in an e-mail sent out by Francis Frangipane that said, "Jesus went through a process of 30 years to reach His full stature, but in just three and a half years, in less than 44 months, Jesus released the disciples to minister in what He was doing. Jesus taught them the Word, but He also imparted the authority to do what He did. Jesus' goal was to release the same level of His ministry to the disciples' ministry through impartation. Even after He died, the effect of impartation was continued through positional seating at the Father's right hand. 'Greater works than these shall you do, because I go to My Father' (see John 14:12). Through the Holy Spirit, Jesus imparted apostolic leadership, which penetrated strength of character, endowment of signs and wonders and confirming authority. Jesus took 12 men, stayed with them just three and a half years, and imparted the very thing He ministered in. It was through this impartation that the disciples changed the world."

As long as I live, I will never forget that night of impartation at Benny Hinn's conference. At that moment I was changed and transformed. At that moment I was released into a greater realm of destiny for my life. Every time we embrace impartation from the Holy Spirit, we are being change in our inner man. We are embracing the working of the Holy Spirit in us.

I share my story with you to provoke a deep hunger within you. Ask God right now, regardless of where you are, for your own divine impartation, your own personal treasure. Are you hungry? Just ask Him. Get ready, here it comes! Let the rock pour out rivers of oil for you, so that your path drips with fresh oil and anointing. (See Job 29:6.)

Keys to sustain and see increase of the anointing:

- *Abide in Him*. (See John 15:5.) A combination of prayer, the Word, and worship equals communion with God.

- Cherish the oil. Honor the Holy Spirit. (See Proverbs 21:20.)

- *Activate*. Use what you have been given. (See Luke 4:18.)

*F*ather, *Thank you for releasing divine impartation, by the power of the Holy Spirit, from You to those who are reading this right now. We are grateful for the oil of the Holy Spirit. Amen!*

CHAPTER 4

Demonstration of Power

A S I shared earlier, I had a powerful experience in 1994 with the Holy Spirit that radically changed my life and ministry. After this encounter, I received a mighty download of the anointing, and one of the first things the Lord began to change was the way I ministered. Remember, I had come to a point in my life when I was tired of seeing powerless ministry. People would come to the altar for prayer, but seemed to leave unchanged. Time after time I had seen this happen. This began my quest when I cried out to the Lord every day from Psalm 63:2, "*So I have looked for You in the sanctuary, to see Your power and Your glory!*" The Holy Spirit first gave me revelation from First Corinthians 2:2 5,

> *For I determined not to know anything among you except Jesus Christ and Him crucified. I was with you in weakness, in fear, and in much trembling. And my speech and my preaching were not with persuasive words of human wisdom, but in demonstration of the Spirit and of power, that your faith should not be in the wisdom of men but in the power of God.*

I will never forget that evening when I was mightily touched and filled with the power of the Holy Spirit! Acts 10:38 says, "*God anointed Jesus of Nazareth with the Holy Spirit and with power, who went about doing good and healing all who were oppressed by the devil, for God was with Him."* Now that is the kind of anointing I wanted to receive from the Lord!

As I read this passage in First Corinthians 2, the Lord spoke to me about ministering out of the Holy Spirit's flow in order to see the anointing of power released in our meetings.

The first thing He shared was to never again minister out of *emotions.* When I would share emotional messages I would get emotional responses at the altar, but the problem was that there was no *power* to change lives. People would leave the same way they came.

In John 6:63 Jesus said, *"It is the Spirit who gives life; the flesh profits nothing. The words that I speak to you are spirit, and they are life."* That was exactly the message the Holy Spirit shared with me that night. I began to understand that I could move and minister out of the power of the precious Holy Spirit and that lives would be transformed.

Second Corinthians 3:17 says, *"Now the Lord is the Spirit, and where the Spirit of the Lord is, there is liberty."* Only the Holy Spirit brings transformation, and only the words anointed by the Holy Spirit will bring life.

HE CAN DO IT THROUGH YOU

He wants to do that for your life. In fact He longs to do that *through* your life. He wants to work through your life "above and beyond anything you could ever do" (see Eph. 3:19-20). Then Jesus will get all the glory. Every believer has the potential to see the impossible become possible by the Holy Spirit's power. The Holy Spirit wants to use our lives to testify of the reality of the Lord by *demonstration*, not by mere words!

The word *demonstrate* used in First Corinthians 2:4 means "to prove; to show; to make evident; to confirm; to manifest." In others words, He wants to prove, show, make evident, confirm, and manifest the Holy Spirit's power through our lives on a day-to-day basis, so that people will once again be in awe of Jesus' mighty name.

The Lord also wants to release power mantles to ministers, so that there will be such great demonstration of the Holy Spirit's power that only Jesus will receive the glory.

At this point I am emphasizing the *demonstration of power*, but if you take notice, First Corinthians 2:4 actually says "*demonstration of the Spirit and power*"! We will dive into the demonstration of the Spirit in the coming chapters. The anointing is not people falling down, however that can be the response to the anointing at times. The anointing is God's tangible manifest presence upon people with Holy Spirit power. God is unlimited, so His anointing has *unlimited power*. Let's look at power now.

> *Now when they saw the boldness of Peter and John, and perceived that they were uneducated and untrained men, they marveled. And they realized that they had been with Jesus. And seeing the man who had been healed standing with them, they could say nothing against it. But when they had commanded them to go aside out of the council, they conferred among themselves, saying, "What shall we do to these men? For, indeed, that a notable miracle has been done through them is evident to all who dwell in Jerusalem, and we cannot deny it"* (Acts 4:13-16).

The Holy Spirit wants to anoint you with power so that you will be a witness for Jesus not in mere words but in demonstrations of His Holy Spirit. He wants to use your life to manifest, prove, and confirm the reality of the unseen realm. He wants to empower your life on a day-to-day basis in your home, in your workplace, in your community, and in everyday living. We must understand that the Lord is beginning to activate His people to move in the supernatural; as a result, we will see the impossible become possible wherever we go.

PAUL MINISTERED BY THE SPIRIT'S POWER

The great apostle Paul is the author of First Corinthians 2:2-5, which I quoted at the beginning of the chapter. What blesses me so much about Paul is that he writes from revelation and understanding. The teaching he received was not something that was taught to him in the natural realm; it was taught by the revelation of Jesus Christ released to him. (See Galatians 1:12.)

Paul was well taught and well educated. We can see through Scripture that he had great natural ability. (See Philippians 3:4-7.) He did not use his own ability, because Paul wanted people to understand that they, too, could operate in a realm of revelation to see a demonstration, not of man's wisdom, but of God's. Paul wasn't trying to flaunt his own analytical ability, but to demonstrate God's power.

ARE YOU HUNGRY?

Do you want to see a greater release of the demonstration of God's power in your life? An emotional response never has eternal value, and the Lord wants to activate His people to live in the reality of the Kingdom. This is done by the anointing.

I believe we are a generation who hungers to walk in the fullness of the Holy Spirit's anointing. Is this your desire? It is God's desire for you! Do you know that the anointing never has to run out from your life? I don't want just yesterday's anointing; I want to learn how to live and plug in day by day into the fresh oil of the Holy Spirit!

The Lord wants to empower the Church to demonstrate the gospel now! I'm not just talking about words, but a demonstration of the Spirit's power—not just in church services, crusades, or revival meetings, but in a daily manifestation of God's power through the believer's life. He wants to increase our influence by the anointing. We can influence in many ways, but I want the anointing to influence. The flesh profits nothing, but the Spirit is eternal.

God wants to do something in the Church. Do you understand that church is more than a building? Church is everyday life. Worship is not just 30 minutes of tuning up the instruments. Worship is a lifestyle. Christianity is not a religion; it's our life— Christ in us and upon us. I believe the Lord wants to open up the heavens and release a greater measure of the anointing on every believer's life right now.

REVIVAL IN ALBUQUERQUE

Ever since that powerful encounter with the Holy Spirit, our ministry has never been the same, praise God! Let me continue with my progressive journey with the Holy Spirit. I was learning the things I just shared with you. The Lord had stirred me up to contend for His power and glory in the sanctuary. He began to display His mighty power demonstrations in our meetings after I received this anointing.

One example of this happened in 1996, when revival broke out in our meetings in Albuquerque, New Mexico, in a place they call "the War Zone." It had so much crime that they patrolled by helicopter—a silent hummer that runs with night gear.

We had started off with only 15 people in the meetings, but after three months the attendance exploded to hundreds. There was such an anointing that some people walked into the facility and immediately hit the floor. Nobody even prayed for them or talked to them. If they were demon-possessed, they fell down and started manifesting.

I held many services during those three months. I did Hispanic services on certain Sunday nights. During the first of these services, preaching through a translator, I said, "Holy Spirit, come!" My translator fell out on the floor with a *bam!* The place was packed, and he was out on the floor. Do you know what I said? "How many want more of Jesus?" The whole place erupted and I said, "That's good enough."

Do you know how the revival really broke open? Once a Catholic man was in the audience. He had been in a head-on collision that had messed him up so badly that the doctors couldn't put his face back together. There was actually a gap from the top of his skull all the way down his cheekbone. It had been like that for years. I was preaching, and all I knew was to say, "Holy Spirit, come!" The next thing I knew, I heard a *boom*, and the man with the gap in his face was on the wooden floor. I hadn't prayed for him or anything. He made a sound as though he was in a lot of pain. I thought, *Man, maybe we need to get that guy off the floor.* It was supposed to be a good time under the anointing, but this guy sounded like he wasn't having a good time.

I'll never forget what happened next. While I was still preaching, he got up. During his time on the floor the Lord had rearranged his face and put it all back together. Praise the Lord! The guy beamed. You could physically see that something had happened. The only thing I knew to do was just keep preaching.

This Catholic man started calling all of his Catholic friends. He called one family whose seven-year-old daughter was scheduled for surgery on a large brain tumor. Because of the size and location of the tumor, the prognosis wasn't good. Even if she came out of the surgery, she wouldn't be the same as before. The next night, this family attended the meeting; the place was packed. I preached favorite Scriptures like Job 29:6, praying, *Holy Spirit, pour out rivers of oil for me*. It always worked.

When you're hungry, you draw on the anointing. When you're really hungry and you get a river of the Holy Spirit coming, do you know that other people get hit by it, too? I asked for what I call "the honey anointing" that night. I call it the honey anointing because it reminds me of the thickness and heaviness of pure honey. It's so sticky that when people touch you, it gets on them. When my wife eats honey with her chicken, there will be a little drop of it on the counter that gets all over me.

I didn't know anything about the girl with the brain tumor. In the middle of preaching, I walked over to where she was sitting. I just put my hand on top of her head while I was preaching. I didn't get a word of knowledge. I didn't even know she was sick, I just felt led to touch her. I was preaching under a river of the anointing. She hit the pew and fell out in her mom's lap. Her face was red.

A few minutes later I heard a commotion, so I looked over there to see the mom and dad crying, and the little girl laughing with joy! She said that after I put my hand on her, she felt something leave her head. All the pain was gone. The next week, before the surgery, new x-rays showed the tumor was gone! Give the Lord praise!

Word started getting out in Albuquerque about the healings, and the next thing you know, the New Agers started coming. I didn't even know what a New Ager was! I approached one lady and said, "In the name of the Lord Jesus." During the preaching, the power of God hit this lady; she fell on the floor, and a demon manifested through her. I just read the Bible and did what the Bible says to do. Jesus said, "Come out. Peace." She coughed seven times. She lay in His peace on that wood floor. She came back the next night. I had just preached for 20 minutes about the anointing. I asked how many wanted it and the whole front filled up.

Every day, for about five days, this lady was right down at the front, and I noticed she brought more people with her each time. They'd come up to the front. I could tell they were a group because when they would get under the power of God, they'd all say, "Aah!" Then they'd be freed.

This lady was one of Albuquerque's New Age teachers. In these meetings, she was radically born again and led everyone in her group to the Lord Jesus. She went from teaching New Age to holding women's Bible studies in Albuquerque for the next several years. Whom the Son sets free is free indeed! Give the Lord glory! I prayed for people, and the Holy Spirit did the rest every night for six months.

MEADVILLE REVIVAL

In 1999, we went to a little town called Meadville, Pennsylvania, where my dear friend Rodney Orsborn lived. He had been calling me every week and saying, "Keith, come up here and do some meetings. We're hungry for the anointing."

I had not yet started holding conferences. I was just pressing in to God. All I knew was that I was hungry for God and I wanted to see the anointing I had read about in the Bible. I was totally convinced that if He could do it in New Testament days, He could do it now. The Book of Hebrews says that Jesus Christ is the same today as He was yesterday, and He is going to be the same forever. What He did then, He wants to do right now. What He did in Capernaum, He wants to do in your city. You can't convince me otherwise.

Is your city the hardest city? Good! If people are hard, then they're miserable, void, and empty. It means they've been trying to find life in what the world has to offer, and they've come up bankrupt. Now we can introduce them to Someone who can give them abundant life.

So I went to Meadville. As in Albuquerque, the meetings began with just a small group of people. The first three days I preached, the preacher said, "Man, we're in revival, Keith. Stay another week." I was thinking, *Dude, you're crazy!*

It surely was revival, though. Some of the people sitting on the pews had never experienced the Lord's presence before. The anointing would come in on them, and they would hold on to the fronts of the pews, their faces looking like they were on a roller coaster. It was pretty funny.

After the second week, we still had the same small group of people. The pastor said, "We're in revival. We need to keep going."

I said, "I've been away from my wife two weeks now, brother."

He said, "No, really. This is revival."

I was thinking, *This isn't the kind of revival I've been in.*

Guess what happened the third week? The meetings exploded! Hundreds of people came—from over 80 cities, 12 states, and 30 different denominations. They stood in line at 5 P.M. to get a seat. We had standing room only for those meetings. A weekend meeting exploded into a ten-week meeting that touched thousands of lives and impacted a region! Signs, wonders, and healings took place in a mighty way.

The warlocks and New Agers began to come, along with people who hadn't been in church for years. People who were going to commit suicide heard about the meeting, and they came and were born again. Some people actually repented to their bosses because of the way they had been treating them. Even now, people who were impacted there come to our meetings and tell us they are still serving the Lord fervently. People send us notes and say, "The Meadville Outpouring changed my life…." They were drawn to the Lord's presence; they were drawn to the anointing.

Our mere words do not draw people, but the anointing does. In Philippians 3:8, the apostle Paul writes that he counts one thing as precious—it's the Holy Spirit, the anointing. Now, Paul knew the Lord. He had had face-to-face encounters with Jesus, but he still hungered to become more intimately and deeply acquainted with Him and His ways.

FAIRFIELD REVIVAL

In Fairfield, Iowa, we saw the same thing. We started meetings that began touching that region. People were saved, delivered, and healed; marriages were restored; and hundreds receiving a fresh anointing of the Holy Spirit. Every weekend for over six months we saw lives transformed and touched by the Holy Spirit's power. Several people from those meetings were launched into powerful ministries. We know of one particular couple who are now doing crusades in Africa, India, and other places because of the fire of revival that hit that small Iowa town.

PROGRESSIVE HEALING

I am amazed that months after our meetings we continue to get testimonies. Healing can be progressive. In one of our meetings was a lady in so much pain that she was taking one thousand milligrams of painkillers each day. She couldn't walk or run. Twenty years on this kind of medication, and she still had constant pain. The Lord instantaneously took away her pain. She threw her cane up in the air and went running around the place.

A year later I went back to this area, and this same lady came running up to me. She jumped up and down and said, "It stuck, it stuck, it stuck!"

I said, "What do you mean, it stuck?"

She said, "You prayed for me when I was on one thousand milligrams of painkillers a day, and the Lord healed me. Look! I'm doing even better now. Both knees had no cartilage or ligaments because they had been eaten away by arthritis and different things. The x-rays showed that within three months, the Lord grew brand-new cartilage and ligaments in my knees!"

At our meetings a few months ago, the Lord gave a word of knowledge about an injured athlete who was present. This man had been a weight lifter but had torn his rotator cuff. He could n't even lift 50 pounds and he was in intense pain. The Lord healed him in that meeting! Recently he approached me at a Benny Hinn conference to report that he's back to lifting 200 plus pounds every day—because of the revelation of Isaiah 53:5, which says that Jesus took our pain.

HUNGER FOR THE FULLNESS

Are you hungry and thirsty for a breakthrough of the anointing? It's OK to be thirsty. In fact, I want to congratulate you, because that's the best place to be. David was the same way. He said, "*My flesh cries out. My soul is thirsty like the desert, being in the desert without a drink. I long to see Your power and Your glory in the sanctuary*" (see Ps. 63:1-2).

I want the Lord to fill me with the fatness of the marrow of His anointing until I'm overflowing and my lips can't help but speak of His lovingkindness. I've got the cure for mumbling and grumbling; it's called the fatness of the marrow, or the anointing. It's the richness of the anointing. The Lord sent leanness of soul into the midst of the Hebrew children because they didn't seek Him anymore and they forgot His works. (See Psalm 106:15.) They got into traditions and religion and performance. They forgot about Him. I want to be lean in the natural, but in the Spirit I want to be so *fat*.

The Holy Spirit wants to do something fresh in this season that's not half a cup, not three-quarters of a cup, but a *full cup*. He wants to bring overflow to the believer's life. Are you ready for the *overflow*? With the overflow you can't help but speak of His lovingkindness, because you're just so full of the anointing.

We're a generation who wants to live daily in the fullness, the perpetual, ceaseless supply of the fresh oil. We want to flow so strongly with the anointing that our paths are literally like butter (see Job 29:6 KJV), and everybody we come near is touched. Isaiah 10:27 says that the anointing destroys yokes and removes burdens. We want to see yokes destroyed and burdens removed by the power of the Holy Spirit so that they never come back. "Whom the Son sets free is free indeed" (see John 8:31). It's the Holy Ghost infusion that explodes to touch the nations.

Our own thinking can keep us from the next level of visitation. One of the worst things I believe we could do is say, "Been there, done that"—this attitude dishonors the Holy Spirit. Today is a new day, and there's no telling what the Holy Spirit wants to do. Honor the Holy Spirit by saying, "Holy Spirit, I honor You. I want to know You even more. I want to dive deeper into the well of salvation. I want to know the depths of You." He's a rich treasure chest full of wisdom and understanding.

ABUNDANT LIVING

I'm totally convinced that the Lord wants to do something extraordinary in every believer's life, because He promised us abundant living. Abundant living doesn't mean having a nice home or cars, even though there's nothing wrong with those things. Abundant life means God is doing things through our lives that are extraordinarily above and beyond what we can do. Do you want the Lord to open up rivers of anointing in your life? By the power of the Holy Spirit you can live in the day-to-day blessing where the extraordinary becomes ordinary.

The precious Lord Jesus really does long for all His dear children to walk in the fullness of Christ, the anointed One, and in the fullness of His anointing. He has promised that He will do this by the power of His Spirit. His anointing is all the power we need, and as we yield and surrender to Him, we will see Him glorified through mighty demonstrations of His power. As you can see, the anointing of God has changed everything about my ministry and life.

I pray the Lord would grant you an expansion of the realm of open heaven you're living in. I'm asking that God would increase the anointing right now, so that wherever you go, an outpouring goes with you. I'm asking for the fire that empowers you to live the Christian life in victory daily. Then you'll be a living epistle, and your life can't help but diffuse and send out a fragrance. The people around you will hear a shofar sound of "Victory! Victory in the Lord and His mighty power! Be strong in the Lord and His mighty power." Amen.

CHAPTER 5

Demonstration of the Spirit

And I, brethren, when I came to you, did not come with excellence of speech or of wisdom declaring to you the testimony of God. For I determined not to know anything among you except Jesus Christ and Him crucified. I was with you in weakness, in fear, and in much trembling. And my speech and my preaching were not with persuasive words of human wisdom, but in demonstration of the Spirit and of power, that your faith should not be in the wisdom of men but in the power of God (1 Corinthians 2:1-5).

UP to this point in my Christian walk, I had been so blessed to be used of the Lord in mighty power. I have shared with you a little of what took place over the course of seven years after times of intense hunger which caused me to press into Psalm 63 and Acts 1:8. My daily cries were, "Where is the glory and power in Your sanctuary?"

The Lord released a powerful anointing in our lives through Pastor Benny Hinn's ministry. My life testifies of the Lord's desire to take ordinary people and do extraordinary things through them. Then He alone receives the glory! I stand in awe of God's goodness. I never thought I would be going around the world preaching the Gospel. What an honor! I am so thankful for His hand upon my life.

HOLY SPIRIT BECKONING

Early in the summer of 2002, I began to feel the Holy Spirit stirring again; it was even deeper than in 1994. He was doing something so deep that I experienced what I like to call the *holy ache*! This is when you're in desperate pursuit of Him. You can't even say that you initiated it; the desire is initiated by Him.

> *So the Lord stirred up the spirit of Zerubbabel the son of Shealtiel, governor of Judah, and the spirit of Joshua the son Jehozadok, the high priest, and the spirit of the remnant of the people; and they came and worked on the house of the Lord of hosts, their God* (Haggai 1:14).

The words *stirred up* mean "to rouse, awaken, excite, raise up; to incite; to arouse to action; to open one's eyes." The word is used 75 times in the Old Testament. It is used to describe how an eagle stirs up its nest (see Deut. 32:11), and to describe how a musical instrument is awakened or warmed up before it is played (see Ps 108:2). It is used twice in Isaiah 50:4; the Lord *awakens* the prophet each morning and *awakens* his ear to hear God's message.

The Lord was arousing my inner man to press in even more. I knew from previous encounters that the Lord was about to show me something new. It was different this time, though, because I wasn't in a place of not seeing God move. This time it was out of a place of desiring to see God do even more.

Jeremiah 33:3 says, "*Call to Me, and I will answer you, and show you great and mighty things, which you do not know.*" This is called *holy desperation!* The Lord initiates the hunger, as He stirs up our spirit, and then we respond by calling out to Him. He answers us by showing us great and hidden mighty things we did not know.

In this context, the word *mighty* means "inaccessible." It means that it was once fortified, fenced in, and we had no access, but now it has been opened up so that we can come in! He gives us "clearance" to come in to a place where He reveals mysteries.

The apostle John was drawn by the Lord to come into a deeper realm of Christ:

> *Behold, I stand at the door and knock. If anyone hears My voice and opens the door, I will come in to him and dine with him, and he with Me. To him who overcomes I will grant to sit with Me on My throne, as I also overcame and sat down with My Father on His throne. He who has an ear, let him hear what the Spirit says to the churches* (Revelation 3:20-22).

Wow! This is a picture of the stirring. Jesus initiates by knocking at the door of our heart. If we *respond in holy hunger* to Him, then He comes in and dines with us. This is a place of communion, of spending time together. Look what happens after this first stirring. Jesus opens a door for John to come before His throne! He says in Revelation 4:1b, "*Come up here, and I will show you things which must take place after this.*" John opens a door at Jesus' invitation, and then Jesus opens a door for John to come up to His throne. He basically says "I'm going to show you great and mighty things."

How many want to partake of the mysteries? This can be multiple levels, for you, your families, your ministry, the Church, and worldwide. But He initiates the fellowship. I love the idea that such close communion was once inaccessible, but now it's accessible by the Spirit of the Lord. We have access to the Father by one Spirit (see Eph. 2:18).

First Corinthians 2:6-10 says there is an ordained wisdom for our age, and that the Holy Spirit, the *Revealer*, wants to reveal it to us. John 16:12-15 says,

> *I still have many things to say to you, but you cannot bear them now. However, when He, the Spirit of truth, has come, He will guide you into all truth; for He will not speak on His own authority, but whatever He hears He will speak; and He will tell you things to come. He will glorify Me, for He will take of what is Mine and declare it to you. All things that the Father has are Mine. Therefore I said that He will take of Mine and declare it to you.*

So the Holy Spirit reveals the things that are to come, the things that we could not bear before, but now we can. The Holy Spirit transmits to you what the Lord is saying. The Father gives it to the Son, and the Son gives it to you through His Spirit!

RESTORATION OF ALL THINGS

The Scriptures declare in Acts 3:21, "[Jesus Christ] *whom heaven must receive until the times of restoration of all things, which God has spoken by the mouth of all His holy prophets since the world began.*" The root word for *restoration* in this verse literally means "to restore back to the original, perfect state before the Fall." This means that everything that was stolen from the Church since the Fall of man is going to be restored back by the Lord. Just like it was before sin entered. Incredible!

This means that all truth in the Word that Jesus purchased for you and me at Calvary, all truth the devil has blinded us from walking in, will be restored back double or even seven times more. (See Exodus 22:7; Proverbs 6:30-31.) One of the Holy Spirit's main ministries is to reveal truth to you as a believer. It's more important for us to embrace truth than to be right or wrong. If we'll always embrace truth, we'll go from wave to wave of His Spirit's move, or from glory to glory in the Lord.

Do you want to see a massive Holy Spirit outpouring? If you research Joel 2:25, you will see what happens first before the Holy Spirit is poured out on all flesh. The first thing is *restoration*. He begins to restore what the canker worm ate. He begins to restore what the thief stole. The restoration releases the outpouring of the Spirit.

The Church has been in restoration since the days of Martin Luther. As you study church history, you will find many instances where lost truths were restored. Would you like to be a forerunner who restores lost truths back to the Church? Most people who were forerunners in their day were called heretics. They didn't become heroes of the faith until about 40 years after they died. Do you understand they were blazing the way for us?

The devil has ravaged people's lives, heritages, cities, and nations with his lies since the Fall, but the restoration of all things will come when the Lord Jesus' Kingdom comes on earth as it is in Heaven. Would you like to be a brave one who restores lost heritages, restores desolate people, cities, regions, and nations to God's original intended plan for them in His Kingdom? If so, take a look at Isaiah 61, because He has anointed us with His Spirit for such things!

BREAKER ANOINTING

Micah 2:13 says that, *"The one who breaks open will come up before them; they will break out, pass through the gate, and go out by it; their king* [Jesus!] *will pass before them, with the Lord at their head."* We can also explain it this way: The Lamb, who is worthy to break open the seals to release the revelation of the Word, broke open the way, and as He broke it open, we now can go through the gate following Him, who is our Head. We get to taste and see that the Lord is good, and then He anoints us as "breakers" who get to break open the way for others, too. I call this the breaker anointing.

Deuteronomy 29:29 says, *"The secret things belong to the Lord our God, but those things which are revealed belong to us and to our children forever, that we may do all the words of this law."* Wow! The exact same word translated "reveal" is used in Amos 3:7, *"Surely the Lord God does nothing, unless He **reveals** His secret to His servants the prophets."* When the Lord reveals a secret, it isn't just for a few; it's for all. Every breakthrough we have experienced, the Lord broke open for us.

He will stir up a forerunner, or a person, or group to follow Him—because they have heard His voice. He breaks through, and they get to break through with Him, and then they lead others. Isaiah 62:10 says, *"Go through, go through the gates! Prepare the way for the people; build up, build up the highway! Take out the stones, lift up a banner for the peoples."* As you're willing to go on, you begin to lay a course for the others to follow.

Don't you want to see the banner of Jesus lifted up over your community or home to be a signal to the lost? Our breakthrough becomes the breakthrough for many. The Lord is the one who initiates breakthrough. When He invites you to come in, you're participating with a breaker anointing. The Christians who have gone on before us, who have plowed, weren't celebrated for what they did. Many were even martyred. But they had tasted something. They refused to shrink back from death but overcame by the blood of the Lamb and the word of their testimony (see Rev. 12:11). As they pressed through (because the Kingdom of God was pressing in), there was *breakthrough*, and you and I get to go through their breakthroughs!

God called on Zerubbabel, the governor of Judah, to do something that looked impossible—to restore and rebuild the temple. The prophet Zechariah had seen the temple in a vision, and God gave him the blueprints for it. The first things God showed Zechariah, via the angel of the Lord, were the gold lamp stand and the two olive trees that dispensed a continual and unending supply of fresh oil to feed the lamp. (See Zechariah 4.)

Why would the Lord show Zechariah the two olive trees and the lamp stand? Why would the Lord say to Zerubbabel, "*Not by might nor by power, but by My Spirit*" (Zech. 4:6)? Also, "*For who has despised the day of small things? For these seven rejoice to see the plumb line in the hand of Zerubbabel*" (Zech. 4:10a). This is showing the release of the Zechariah *breaker generation* whose hands were anointed with fresh oil, who are called "sons of fresh oil" because they lived in a perpetual, ceaseless supply of the Holy Spirit for their lives! (I will go into this text on Zechariah and the lamp stand in more detail in another chapter of this book.)

It's so important for this generation to hear the word of the Lord, because some of the forerunners in past moves of God didn't finish the race well. Much of their generation didn't receive what they were walking in.

The Lord has recently been drawing attention to forerunners like the Maria Woodworth-Etters, the Kathryn Kuhlmans, the Jack Coes, and all the wonderful greats who have dug wells and had major breakthroughs; but we're not seeing those levels in the

Western church today. These breakthroughs weren't just for that generation, but for *all* generations. The Bible says, "*to us and to our children forever*" (Deut. 29:29). So their breakthrough can be your breakthrough. In fact, every believer has the opportunity to drink from that well; and once you drink from the well, you know that "*out of* [your] *belly shall flow rivers of living water*" (see John 7:38 KJV).

Would you like to establish those breakthroughs in your life and in the church? You are the Church, and it is your blessing. Jesus broke the way open to reveal every truth. Now He says, "When the Revealer reveals, it's for the children's children." There is an anointing to restore to the Church lost inheritances that have been lying dormant for years. He says, "I'm going to favor this generation. What was not flowing will now flow, and everybody will drink from that well."

I share all this to bring out that the Lord is constantly restoring to the Church everything He intended for us. Those who have gone before us have had breakthroughs, and their breakthroughs have become our breakthroughs, and to all generations. The Lord is releasing many things to this generation that will catapult us into seeing God's Kingdom come mightily upon the earth.

SPIRIT OF BURNING

During 2002 when I began sensing this deep drawing of the Holy Spirit, I knew that I was about to meet with Him, and He was going to release something I did not know. I pressed in, prayed, and read the Word. After a few weeks of doing this, one day in my office I suddenly fell down and began to pray in the Spirit very intensely.

I said, "Lord, search and try me; if You find anything in my life that is not pleasing to You or is keeping me from what You have, please Lord, send Your holy fire!" All of sudden the fire of God came and rested upon me; for hours I lay on the floor under judgment and the spirit of burning.

Isaiah 4:4 describes something like this: "*When the Lord has washed away the filth of the daughters of Zion, and purged the blood of Jerusalem from her midst, by the spirit of judgment and by the spirit of burning….*" The Lord was making judgment against everything in me that was the enemy of my soul. The Spirit burned it up and replaced it with holy zeal! I do what I do because the Lord's passion burns like fire in my bones! Then I had the encounter during the school of revival that released me into a series of events that I shared in Chapter 1.

Please notice the phrase "*demonstration of the Spirit and power*" in First Corinthians 2:4. I had seen a great release of the demonstration of power, but now the Lord was about to teach me and release to me the demonstration of the Spirit. Again, the word *demonstration* means "to prove; to show; to make evident; to confirm; to manifest." One of the things the Lord put on my heart to pray during this time of pressing in was this: "Holy Spirit, I want to know You like Jesus knows You!" This statement was released in me so that I would begin calling out to Him. That is when I received the revelation from Isaiah 11:2 and Revelation 4:5 on the seven Spirits of God.

JESUS' ANOINTING

Jesus did not minister out of a finite measure of the Holy Spirit and power when He lived on earth; He knew the unlimited anointing of the Holy Spirit. John 3:34 shows us this: "*For He whom God has sent speaks the words of God, for God does not give the Spirit by measure.*" He received the fullness of the Holy Spirit. This happened as he was baptized by John the Baptist in

Mark 1:10, "*And immediately, coming up from the water, He saw the heavens parting and the Spirit descending upon Him like a dove.*" The word *parting* means "out of a torn Heaven." He ministered from out of an open Heaven. So with the fullness of the Holy Spirit, there was no lack, no measure; He knew the fullness.

Do you know what an open Heaven is? It means no restrictions between you and God. Anything can happen. Times are coming where Heaven is going to open up wide. The preaching and the power of the Word will be like the events of Acts chapter 2. There will be outpourings on whole cities, and cities will be changed in a day!

Are you ready for open Heavens in your life, in your ministry, in your church, and in your city? I believe that we're about to see extraordinary things become ordinary because by living in Him, we can live under an open Heaven. The Lord wants to open Heaven over your life.

Acts 10:38 says, "*God anointed Jesus of Nazareth with the Holy Spirit and with power, who went about doing good and healing all who were oppressed by the devil, for God was with Him.*" Jesus ministered in demonstrations of the Spirit and power. He not only revealed great power, but He ministered out of the sevenfold Holy Spirit. Isaiah 11:1-2 describes the fullness of the Holy Spirit Jesus operated under:

> *There shall come forth a Rod from the stem of Jesse, and a Branch shall grow of his roots. The Spirit of the Lord shall rest upon Him, the Spirit of wisdom and understanding, the Spirit of counsel and might, the Spirit of knowledge and of the fear of the Lord.*

Jesus ministered in a mighty anointing of power but also with unlimited flow of the sevenfold Holy Spirit. The *manifest Presence of the Spirit of the Lord was upon Him* in such a way that people just sought to touch Him. He moved in such *wisdom* that people marveled. He moved in such *understanding* of God's ways that the wisest wondered where He got such understanding. He revealed the *counsel* of God that caused many to literally be overwhelmed; the *might* of God was demonstrated in a great way as He never wavered but lived in God's strength; the manifestation of the *power* of God through His life got the attention of whole cities. He operated out the spirit of *knowledge* to such a degree that many were speechless in their accusations against Him; and He so revealed the Father that it caused the *fear of the Lord* to grip the hearts of many.

Revelation 3:1 says of Jesus, "*These things says He who has the seven Spirits of God and the seven stars.*" Jesus has the sevenfold Holy Spirit, and He Himself said in John 20:21, "*Peace to you! As the Father has sent Me, I also send you.*" We can see the Lord wants us to minister in the same manner. He said that those who believe in Him will do even greater things than He did (see John 14:12). Right after He shared this, He went on to speak of the Holy Spirit in John 14:16-17. The Holy Spirit is the reason we will do the greater works!

Ephesians 1:22-23 says, "*And He put all things under His feet, and gave Him to be head over all things to the church, which is His body, the fullness of Him who fills all in all.*" Wow! It says that the Church is the *fullness* of Him who fills all in all. He who has everything under His feet is our Head. As we dwell together in unity as shown in Psalm 133:1-3, we will operate in the fullness of His anointing.

Now if you look at Romans 11:16-17, you'll see that you and I are part of a holy "lump." When you begin to allow the nature and character of God to manifest and be predominant, you'll live a holy life *because He is holy*. This passage goes on to say that we've been grafted into the olive tree—Christ. In a tree, a branch receives the same flow as the tree it is grafted into. Jesus received the anointing without measure. So the fullness of the Holy Spirit came and rested upon Him and never left. Now we are plugged into Him, so we can receive the same unlimited anointing! Because He did, we can, too. Apart from Him we can do nothing. Because He has an open Heaven, then the believer can enjoy the open Heaven, too. His blood paved the way, so we can have unlimited access to God's throne, we can live under an open Heaven, and we can know unlimited anointing of the sevenfold Spirit of God. My heart's cry is, "Receive the reward of Your suffering, Jesus, and let us all walk in the fullness of the Holy Spirit, for Your glory!"

The Church is about to have this great truth restored: it is His presence that releases power. So many times we chase only power. We should seek His holy presence—then His power will flow.

Now watch what happened as Jesus received the anointing. He never sinned. He went through it all and He never failed. So when the Holy Spirit came upon Jesus, He came with a full measure, nothing withheld. Then Jesus went to the wilderness to be tested for 40 days, the length representing a *probated time*. Jesus prevailed in only 40 days of testing, and He didn't fall into sin even once, so He came out in power and victory. When Jesus went to the Cross, one of the most glorious and wonderful things took place. It was the intention of the Lord God to so restore the heart of the Father toward you and me, that we would be able to walk in this realm. God wants you to walk in the fullness because Jesus said, "I'm going to send you out as the Father sent Me." Praise the Lord!

RIVERS OF THE HOLY SPIRIT

In John 7:38-39 Jesus said, "*He who believes in Me, as the Scripture has said, out of his heart will flow rivers of living water.' But this He spoke concerning the Spirit, whom those believing in Him would receive; for the Holy Spirit was not yet given, because Jesus was not yet glorified."* Rivers is not a drip, or squirt, nor a stream; it represents continuous flow. This is not just one river, but multiple rivers. It means multiple flows of the Holy Spirit! It means a river of the Spirit of the Lord, of wisdom, of understanding, of counsel, of might, of knowledge and of the fear of the Lord.

Job 29:6 says, *"When my steps were bathed with cream [butter, fatness], and the rock poured out rivers of oil for me!"* Wow! Jesus, being the Rock, poured out rivers of oil, representing the Holy Spirit.

As we minister out of an open Heaven, just like Jesus did, we will see rivers. This means we minister out of "throne ministry" like Jesus did when He saw what the Father was doing. Revelation 4:5 says, *And from the throne proceeded lightnings, thunderings, and voices. Seven lamps of fire were burning before the throne, which are the seven Spirits of God."* Where are the seven Spirits? They are before the Throne. There is only one Holy Spirit but multiple flows or functions or demonstration of the Spirit of God.

Revelation opens with, *"Grace to you and peace from Him who is and who was and who is to come, and from the seven Spirits who are before His throne"* (Rev. 1:4). Again, we see the seven Spirits are before His throne. So an open Heaven is ministering from His throne. Jesus said, *"If anyone hears My voice and opens the door, I will come in to him and dine with him, and he with Me. To him who overcomes I will grant to sit with Me on My throne, as I also overcame and sat down with My Father on His throne."* (Rev 3:20b-21).

The Lord wants to break out rivers of the demonstrations of the Holy Spirit through your life so that people will not look to you, but to *Him*. He desires you to lead a demonstration of the

Spirit-filled, Spirit-led life. *"For the earnest expectation of the creation eagerly waits for the revealing of the sons of God"* (Rom. 8:19). Mature sons and daughters who know their God will do great exploits above and beyond anything we have seen or heard so that Jesus will get all the glory. (See Romans 8:14; Daniel 11:32; Ephesians 3:20-21.)

Remember, there's only one Holy Spirit but seven expressions, functions, or flows of the Holy Spirit. Seven means *fullness* and *completion*. In the Bible it also means *perfection*. The Lord is raising up a people who walk and live in His Spirit's fullness that will glorify the Lord in a mighty way. That is why He is doing such a deep work in His people and is sending His messengers of fire to burn up all that isn't of Him.

Why don't you invite the Lord to demonstrate the Spirit of the Lord through your life—not in word only, but in a demonstration of the Spirit that will cause people to declare that surely God is with you? Only God could do such a thing.

Recall that the word *demonstration* means "to prove, to show, to make evident, to confirm, to manifest." The Holy Spirit wants to do all of this through your life. He is initiating with you right now! He is stirring you up to call unto Him so that He will show you His mysteries of the Kingdom, and to show you Himself. It was His idea for His people to move in the fullness of the Holy Spirit. Do you want what He's offering?

If you agree with me, let's pray this prayer together:

We want to know You, Holy Spirit, just like Jesus knows You. We want to know You in a mighty way. You said that if we ask anything in Your name, You will do it. We ask You, wonderful Jesus, that we could know the

Holy Spirit like You do and to live and operate out of an open Heaven just like You did on earth as a man. We ask this that You will be glorified through us! Amen.

CHAPTER 6

Seven Spirits As Seen in the Lampstand

IN the traditional Jewish tabernacle, God had instructed that there always be lampstands in the Holy Place, to bring *illumination*. The lamps were oil lights, not candles, and they were never to be extinguished. (See Leviticus 24:1-4.) They illumined the Holy Place so that the priests could walk and minister in the light, and so they could see the showbread which was placed on the altar (in some Bible translations called "Bread of the Presence"). Every morning and evening, the priests tended to the lamps—trimming wicks, taking away ashes, and supplying the oil to keep the lamps continually burning.

Traditionally the lampstands symbolized God's guidance and revelation through His Word. They also speak of Jesus, the light of the world. Salvation also is as a lamp that burns, and the Lord will not hold His peace or rest until the brilliancy of the salvation lamp goes to the nations. (See Psalm 119:105; John 8:12; Isaiah 62:1.)

The oil in the lamps symbolized the anointing of the Holy Spirit, the source of power that illumines the Church. The showbread is a metaphor for the Word of God, our daily bread. The Holy Spirit illuminates the Word, just as the lamplight shone on the showbread. The lamp oil makes our faces shine.

The lampstand signifies the Church. (See Matthew 4:4; Psalm 104:15b; Revelation 1:20.)

There are several references to lampstands (sometimes called candlesticks) in both Old and New Testaments that are, in fact metaphorical: the lampstand in John's heavenly vision, the lampstand in Moses' tabernacle, and the lampstand in Zechariah's fifth vision. (See Revelation 4:5; Exodus 25:31-40; Zechariah 4:2.) These three occurrences symbolize the fullness of the Holy Spirit, the seven Spirits of God referenced in Isaiah 11:2.

ZECHARIAH'S VISION

Now the angel who talked with me came back and wakened me, as a man who is wakened out of his sleep. And he said to me, "What do you see?" So I said, "I am looking, and there is a lampstand of solid gold with a bowl on top of it, and on the stand seven lamps with seven pipes to the seven lamps. Two olive trees are by it, one at the right of the bowl and the other at its left." So I answered and spoke to the angel who talked with me, saying, "What are these, my Lord?" …"This is the word of the Lord to Zerubbabel: 'Not by might nor by power, but by My Spirit,' says the Lord of hosts. 'Who are you, O great mountain? Before Zerubbabel you shall become a plain! And he shall bring forth the capstone with shouts of "Grace, grace to it!"'" Moreover the word of the Lord came to me, saying: "The hands of Zerubbabel have laid the foundation of this temple; his hands shall also finish it. Then you will know that the Lord of hosts has sent Me to you. For who has despised the day of small things? For these seven rejoice to see the plumb line in the hand of Zerubbabel. They are the eyes of the Lord, which scan

*to and fro throughout the whole earth."....And I further
answered and said to him, "What are these two olive
branches that drip into the receptacles of the two gold
pipes from which the golden oil drains?" Then he
answered me and said..."These are the two anointed
ones, who stand beside the Lord of the whole earth"*
(Zechariah 4:1-14).

God gave Zechariah a vision of the golden lampstand in the
temple. Since Zechariah and his people were there to rebuild the
temple, it made sense that God spoke to them in temple images.
The meaning of the vision was to show how Zerubbabel, the governor of Judah, would accomplish the overwhelming work of
rebuilding the temple, by the *Spirit of God*. No doubt it was a
monumental task, and Zerubbabel may have been discouraged.

The lampstand God showed Zechariah represented the full
ministry of the Holy Spirit. God wanted to assure Zerubbabel (via
Zechariah) that the Holy Spirit would continually supply his
needs as he embarked on the enormous building project.
Zerubbabel would not rebuild the temple by his own strength or
ability, but by God's. He could draw on the endless supply of
resources supplied by the sevenfold Spirits of God.

God wants His supply and our reliance on the sevenfold flow
of the Holy Spirit to be *continual*. The work of rebuilding the
temple was so massive it seemed like a great mountain. God
promised that by the fullness of His Spirit, that great mountain
will be leveled into a plain.

Zechariah's vision in Zechariah 4:1-14 adds significant detail
to the metaphorical tabernacle candlestick. He saw a solid gold
lampstand with seven pipes and seven lamps. Two olive trees
dripped oil into a bowl, and the bowl, like a fountain, dripped oil
into the seven pipes. The oil flowed from the pipes into the

seven lamps that burned continuously in the tabernacle. It was a never ending supply of oil.

GRAFTED TO THE OLIVE TREE

The number seven biblically signifies fullness or completion. Here we see a lampstand with seven pipes tapped into a perpetual oil source, two olive trees. The pipes represent seven paths (seven Spirits of God) through which the oil (Holy Spirit) flows. I believe the two olive trees represent the Spirit and the Word. This is a metaphorical image of the Body of Christ plugged into the fullness of the sevenfold flow of the Holy Spirit. Tapping into the source releases the unlimited anointing (fresh oil) of the Holy Spirit. (See John 3:34.)

Legendary evangelist, apostle of faith, and Christian hero Smith Wigglesworth (1859-1947) experienced a prophetic vision where he saw two great revivals sweep across the world. The first, known as the "Word Movement," occurred during the 1970s and the second, "Spirit Revival," came later, in the 1990s. However, in this vision, he saw something much bigger and more powerful that was to happen *following* these two revivals. He saw a massive harvest that would cover the earth, and it would happen when the Word and the Spirit (or anointing) were "married." Unfortunately, he died before he saw any of these events. I believe we're in that time of massive harvest right now!

The foundation of the Bible is very important, but we need to live by the *living* Word daily (see Heb. 4:12). My friend Bill Johnson says, "Faith doesn't come by what you have already heard, it comes by what you are presently *hearing*." If there were ever a time that the Church needs eyes to see and ears to hear what the Spirit is saying, that time is now. God wants us to live daily with our spiritual ears open and eyes illuminated. We can, when we tap into the fullness of the Holy Spirit, fresh oil, every day.

Without oil, there is no flame. Without oil, there is no flow. Apart from Him, the fresh oil, we can do nothing (see John 15:5). When we plug into the source, we're changed and transformed; we walk in purity and holiness before the Lord. He replenishes the oil when we stay plugged into Him. The more we allow the working of the Holy Spirit, the more we embrace His work, and the more we allow Him liberty in our life. These things transform us, from glory to glory to glory into His image.

As believers, we've been grafted in among these olive trees (see Rom. 11:17) and we've become partakers of the root and fatness, the continual flow of the rich flourishing oil. We remain strong as we partake of the oil, and remain grafted and plugged into the flow: *"But my horn You have exalted like a wild ox; I have been anointed with fresh oil"* (Ps. 92:10). Anointed in this context means *overflow*, and horn signifies *strength*. When we function and operate in the full expression of the sevenfold Spirit of God, we'll walk in fresh oil every day. When we remain plugged into Jesus, the Vine, we will be fruitful.

TAPPING INTO ENDLESS SUPPLY

We need fresh oil! We can't live in last week's supply of oil, or the seven flames will die. We need to tap into the ceaseless supply of His fresh oil from the Spirit and the Word daily, and it is available to us now through the "pipes" of the seven Spirits of God!

The lampstand of Zechariah's vision had a center pipe with six other pipes tapped into it. Six represents the number of *man*—add the center pipe, and there are seven. Christ symbolizes the center pipe, because He is the mediator between God and us (see 1 Tim. 2:5). Christ is the center, the divine nature, and all of the other pipes flow out of that one. We cannot have the fullness of the oil without tapping into the center pipe of the lampstand.

From the center pipe, the three pairs of pipes went outward on opposite sides. The three pairs represent the three pairings of flows of the Holy Spirit as mentioned in Isaiah 11:2: wisdom and understanding, counsel and might, and knowledge and the fear of the Lord. Add to these six *"the Spirit of God upon,"* (Presence of Christ), and there are seven. We will take a closer look at each of these seven flows in later chapters.

GRACE, GRACE BY HIS SPIRIT

Next, the angel explains to Zechariah *"This is the Word of the Lord to Zerubbabel: 'Not by might, nor by power, but by My Spirit,' says the Lord of hosts. 'Who are you, O great mountain? Before Zerubbabel, you shall become a plain!'"* In other words, Not by your might, not by your power, not by your strength, but by the Holy Spirit. This is how it's going to happen. You're going to begin to move in the function and fullness of the Holy Spirit, and then grace will be released.

"The hands of Zerubbabel have laid the foundation of this temple; his hands shall also finish it. Then you will know that the Lord of hosts has sent Me to you. For who has despised the day of small things?" Don't despise small beginnings, because you are going to be a finisher like Zerubbabel: *"These seven have rejoiced to see the plumb line in the hands of Zerubbabel."*

GREAT GRACE AND FRESH OIL

The true meaning of the word *Christian* translates as a "little anointed one." *Christ* means *"anointed one,"* so a Christian is a *follower of Christ and His anointing.* Jesus was anointed with the Spirit *without measure* (see John 3:34), so if we are to follow Him, we too are to be anointed with His same unlimited anointing!

The great grace of the Lord is what will accomplish this move of the seven Spirits of God flowing through the Church. It is His grace alone! The mountains referred to in Zechariah 4 represent giants or enemies that stand in the way of the Kingdom of God. His grace will flatten every mountain, praise the Lord! Many mountains will come down.

The Lord is raising up a generation who have pure fresh oil dripping from their hands. *"What are these two olive branches that drip into the receptacles* [into the hands of] ?" The *"two anointed ones"* in the original Hebrew translation signify *sons of fresh, pure oil.* This new generation will live not in yesterday's oil, but in the daily fresh anointing of the Holy Spirit.

Do you want to wake up every day with fresh oil dripping from your hands? The Lord wants you not only filled with fresh oil, but also overflowing with oil to affect people all around you for the Kingdom. We are entering into a new time, a wonderful time in the Lord, into the unlimited anointing of the Holy Spirit. As you walk in His fullness, you will walk in the fullness of the ministry of Jesus. Jesus ministered in such a wonderful way, didn't He? He is the same today as He was yesterday, and He will be the same tomorrow (see Heb. 13:8). Don't you want an anointing of fresh oil every day, strengthening your inner man so you can walk out the fullness of your destiny to glorify Jesus mightily all through the land? When your hands drip with fresh oil you can lay hands on people for healing. God created those hands so that

He could use them. He says every believer is to lay hands on the sick, and they will recover! (See Mark 16:18.)

What the Lord is showing us in Zechariah 4 is a heavenly blueprint or pattern for the Church. He tells us to die to ourselves, to come out of our own perceived strength and perceived power, and live in His ability.

This will release great grace to see every mountain of opposition torn down. The grace of the Lord is a supernatural endowment of the favor of the Lord. What you couldn't do for yourself He does for you!

He tells us to live in grace, and to rejoice with the seven. We are to embrace the small things, knowing they will become bigger. We don't have to operate on yesterday's anointing, but we can live in the perpetual, ceaseless supply of the unlimited daily anointing. We can plug into the Word, the living Word, Christ, *and* the unlimited anointing.

BUILDING FROM A HEAVENLY BLUEPRINT

Exodus 25:31-39 examines God's heavenly pattern for the lampstand in Moses' tabernacle:

> *You shall also make a lampstand of pure gold; the lampstand shall be of hammered work. Its shaft, its branches, its bowls, its ornamental knobs, and flowers shall be of one piece. And six branches shall come out of its sides: three branches of the lampstand out of one side, and three branches of the lampstand out of the other side. Three bowls shall be made like almond blossoms on one branch, with an ornamental knob and a flower, and three bowls made like almond blossoms on the other branch, with an ornamental knob and a*

flower—and so for the six branches that come out of the lampstand. On the lampstand itself four bowls shall be made like almond blossoms, each with its ornamental knob and flower. And there shall be a knob under the first two branches of the same, a knob under the second two branches of the same, and a knob under the third two branches of the same, according to the six branches that extend from the lampstand. Their knobs and their branches shall be of one piece; all of it shall be one hammered piece of pure gold. You shall make seven lamps for it, and they shall arrange its lamps so that they give light in front of it. And its wick-trimmers and their trays shall be of pure gold. It shall be made of a talent of pure gold, with all these utensils.

Nothing even remotely similar had ever been built. There were no other pattern sources or resources for the lampstand. Moses had to trust the pattern God gave him.

The Lord wants to give new things to the Church now, too, so we don't look like the entities of the world. Patterns that come straight down from Heaven are unique, astonishing, and new. When we build from heavenly blueprints, we confound the principalities of the earth and release the manifold wisdom of God.

FRUITS AND GIFTS OF THE SPIRIT MANIFEST

As in Zechariah's vision, the lampstand in Moses' tabernacle had seven pipes, which symbolized the seven Spirits of God. However, this lampstand also had nine different ornaments on the pipes: three flowers, three knobs, and three almond blossom-shaped bowls. Those nine items represent the *nine fruits* described in Galatians 5:22-23, and the *nine gifts* of the Holy Spirit examined in First Corinthians 12:8-10.

When we flow in the seven Spirits of God, the world will see the fruits and gifts of the Spirit flow through us as never before. The world will see a mighty demonstration of God's power, wisdom, and might. If the world ever needed to see the fruit of the Holy Spirit, it is now.

DIVINE GOVERNMENT

On the lampstand were 12 ornaments representing the divine government of the Lord (biblically, the number 12 typifies government: the 12 tribes of Israel, the 12 elders before the throne, and the 12 apostles). There were four almond blossoms, four knobs, and four flowers. The government rests on His shoulders (see Isa. 9:6). As the zeal of the Lord increases, the zeal and passion of God increase in us as well. This in turn results in the increase of God's government, with no end. It is apparent to me that there is a restoration of God's government back to the Church.

CHRIST'S DIVINE NATURE

"You shall also make a lampstand of pure gold. The lampstand shall be of hammered work." Do you think they took each pipe, cut them out, and then welded them together? No! The Lord was specific that it was not to be molded. They had to hammer it into a lampstand from one solid piece of gold. The craftsperson would need divine wisdom to create this beautiful piece.

In Second Peter 1:3-9, the apostle writes that we may be partakers of His divine nature by His divine power, but the process involves challenges that require patience and longsuffering. The tempering work of the Holy Spirit brings forth a divine union of the stature of Christ in us, so that we will begin to flow with the sevenfold Spirit of God through our lives. It took a lot of hammering to mold the Lamp stand. As lights on the hill (see Matt. 5:14), we're going to have to go through some transformation too. However, God promises us the fullness of the Holy Spirit, and when we flow in the sevenfold flow, there will be no limitations.

The center shaft of the lampstand is Jesus. He is the mediator, the One from whom flows oil to give light. The branches are connected. This signifies the divine union with Christ that brings the flow of oil to the six branches.

As Christians, we have received the Holy Spirit of God, whose mission it is to bring forth the nature of Him who has come to dwell in us. He enables us to become partakers of the sevenfold Spirit of God. Just as in the lampstand, we have six branches and one center pipe, the number six again represents the number of man, but with one being Jesus. There are a total of seven then, which means *perfection, fullness, or completeness*. In this it also represents union with Christ. It is no longer I who lives, but He who lives in me. We become one with Him. Apart from Him, we can do nothing. All of the pipes: wisdom and understanding, counsel and might, and knowledge and the fear of the Lord are dependent on the center pipe, Jesus. We must stay plugged into the center pipe, the presence of Jesus; because communion with Him will release fresh oil and fresh anointing and keep the seven flames burning in our lives.

The lampstand was a shadow of what was to come. Through divine union with the Holy Spirit, we become partakers of His divine nature. We know that He received the Spirit of the Lord without measure. Jesus received the fullness of the seven Spirits of God (see Rev. 3:1). He is the head (see Eph. 1:22-23), and the unlimited anointing was poured out upon Him. That same unlimited anointing is for us today.

WE ARE BURNING LAMPS

It is clear from Revelation 4:5, that the burning lampstand and His seven Spirits are one and the same: "*And from the throne came flashes of lightning and the rumble of thunder. And in front of the throne were seven lampstands with burning flames. They are the seven spirits of God*" (NLT).

All of the lampstands we have covered so far are the same; they are God's lampstands. We are the lampstand, and when we plug into the fullness of the seven Spirits of God, we are that glorious burning lamp that stands before the throne in the presence of the Father.

SEATED IN HEAVENLY PLACES

Every spiritual blessing has been given to us in the heavenly places (Eph.1:3). We are not going to grovel in the earthly realm, but we are going to be seated in the heavenly places with the Lord. Every believer will be ministering out of the throne room.

What flows out of the throne room? Rivers flow. What was before the throne? These seven functions or operations of the Holy Spirit always come in pairs after the Spirit of the Lord upon us. I believe the pairing ties in somehow to the pairing of the olive trees Zerubbabel saw in his vision. Counsel pairs with might, wisdom with understanding, and knowledge of the Lord with the fear of the Lord. It's awesome! By these pairings, His divine power, and the fullness of the Holy Spirit, we will be partakers of His divine nature.

The Lord told me, "I am building stature and strength in my people for what I am about to do." We will need a deep work of strength in our inner man and the stature of Christ in us for this realm of glory that He is about to release. We will walk in it and fulfill the destiny of God for our lives. Many saints have been going through difficult trials, but it is just the hammering of the Lord. Like the lamp, we are not cut; we are hammered from one solid piece of gold, the gold that represents Jesus.

A time is coming when we will not want anything but the heart and mind of the Father. We are going through a transformation that we have to embrace, as Paul stresses in Colossians 1:28-29: "*Him we preach, warning every man and teaching every man in all wisdom, that we may present every man perfect in Christ Jesus. To this end I also labor striving according to His working which works in me mightily.*"

Are you hungry for transformation? I know I am. I want to know, hear, see, and be like Jesus. Embrace His work in you so that He can work through you mightily. Embrace the ministry of the Holy Spirit and allow the sevenfold flow to manifest in your life.

As we become one in this divine union, we become obedient to His voice. We engage spirit to Spirit, and this engages the King and enthrones Him in the kingdom of our hearts. When we plug into the center pipe, Jesus the living Word, we receive the fresh oil of Psalm 92:10. The anointing pours into the vat, and we become partakers of that rich flow of the unlimited anointing of the Holy Spirit.

Fresh oil feeds the flames—the seven flames atop the seven pipes. It has to be a continuous flow of oil for the seven flames to burn. We trim the wick and replenish the oil in perpetual communion with Him, and the flame burns in divine union with Him. As we advance in the flow of the sevenfold Spirits of God, the fullness of the Holy Spirit, the flow increases. The greater the flow of oil, the greater the flame; the greater the flame, the greater the favor and influence.

SEVEN SPIRITS OF GOD OVERVIEW

The Holy Spirit wants to bring forth the mature stature of Christ in us through the *sevenfold* functions of His Spirit flowing through us. The seven Spirits of God bestow on us a perpetual flow of His manifest *presence, wisdom and understanding, counsel* and *might, knowledge* and *fear of the Lord.*

The first of the sevenfold operation of the Holy Spirit is the Spirit of the Lord *upon.* This speaks of the Lord resting upon us and covering us with His Holy presence. In Mark 9:2-7, we read about the Lord's transfiguration accompanied by God's holy Presence. We are to be clothed with His presence (see Gal. 3:27). In Acts 10:38, we see how God anointed Jesus with the Holy Spirit and with power, but with the Holy Spirit *upon* Him.

The second Spirit, *wisdom*, is creative ability to do the impossible; it puts the *wow* factor into our works. It is ability beyond our own ability. It is God's thoughts and ideas in action.

The Spirit of *understanding* partners with wisdom to help us understand how to mobilize and implement heavenly blueprints and patterns. It is putting two and two together and making it happen. The Spirit of understanding also helps us articulate the revelation of His Word that we have been shown. Without understanding, we won't know what to do with those heavenly blueprints. In Ephesians 1:17-19 Paul explains what a partnership of wisdom and understanding does:

that the God of our Lord Jesus Christ, the Father of
glory, may give to you the spirit of wisdom and revela-
tion in the knowledge of Him, the eyes of your under-
standing being enlightened; that you may know what is
the hope of His calling, what are the riches of the glory
of His inheritance in the saints, and what is the exceed-
ing greatness of His power toward us who believe,
according to the working of His mighty power.

The Spirit of *counsel* is engaging the One who is the Alpha and the Omega. It is listening for and heeding His counsel. The counsel of the Lord stands forever. As we build by His heavenly plans, God releases fresh flows of His counsel, His thoughts, and the intents of His heart.

Counsel then releases the *might* of God to impart vigor, power, strength, and the anointing to see His divine plans through to fruition. With the might of God, we won't just look for the finger of God or His hand; we will look for His arm—unlimited power and strength! God's might and power are always associated with counsel The prophet Isaiah called Him *Wonderful, Counselor,* and *Mighty God.* We never flow in God's might or power without His wonderful counsel.

The Spirit of *knowledge* of the Lord is when we come into that place of the deep thoughts of God. It is the place of knowing Him—not just His counsel, wisdom, or understanding—but an intimate knowledge of *Him.* Knowledge of Him releases understanding, wisdom, counsel, and might. As we grow in His knowledge, peace and grace multiply, as does our humility. As we increase in our knowledge of His vastness, His depth, His greatness, His awesomeness, His majestic Splendor, we sever limitations, and the impossible becomes possible; the ordinary, extraordinary. In the knowledge of these things, we embrace His counsel with joy. We celebrate wisdom because we know that He can do all things.

As the Spirit of knowledge flows, it releases a deep and reverent *fear of the Lord*. Nothing will foster this godly fear like knowledge of His awesome attributes and His sovereign majesty. Knowledge of who He really is brings to a holy fear that takes us to a completely new spiritual level.

Without the sevenfold Spirits of God operating in our lives, we succumb to our natural limitations. God offers us supernatural ability and power to fulfill our destinies and His plans for us with unlimited resources. God will partner with us, as He did with Zerubbabel and Moses, to confound the world. God gave Zerubbabel and Moses the full measure of the Holy Spirit and they flowed in a constant river of wisdom and understanding, counsel and might, knowledge and reverent fear of the Lord.

God spoke great words of encouragement to Zerubbabel through the vision He gave Zechariah, and He speaks those same words even now to the building of His living temple, the Body of Christ.

Child of God, remember these words. God has pledged His Word that this temple shall be finished. Salvation is as a lamp that burns and the Lord will not hold His peace or rest until the brilliancy of the salvation lamp goes to the nations. Let us never lose that vision. This is the work of the sevenfold flow of God, the oil of the Spirit flowing through us. This is the secret of our power and the fulfillment of salvation to the nations.

CHAPTER 7

Wells of the Seven

IN the story of Isaac's re-digging the wells of his father Abraham, we see a powerful picture of the sevenfold Spirit of God. Isaac opens seven wells, which illustrate the opening of the seven rivers of the Holy Spirit. It is from these unhindered seven flows that the Church will come into the fullness of her destiny.

THE VASTNESS OF GOD

Before we get into Genesis 26 and the re-digging of the wells, let's take a look at Revelation 1:8, "*I am the Alpha and the Omega, the Beginning and the End,*" *says the Lord,* "*who is and who was and who is to come, the Almighty.*" In this season God is increasing our ability to behold His vastness. He's revealing to us just how great and powerful He is, so we can begin to see and believe what seems impossible.

Isaiah 46:10 expresses the idea that God saw all of history before it ever started. He was already there! He's *that* big. Hebrews 13:8 says, "*Jesus Christ is the same yesterday, today, and forever*"— Jesus is, He was, and He is to come. I want to bring out these three different aspects of how Jesus reveals His truths to the Church through a process I call "re-digging the wells of the fathers." It is a key to seeing the Kingdom come in fullness. What exactly does this re-digging mean?

RE-DIGGING THE FATHER'S WELLS

"Now the Philistines had stopped up all the wells which his father's servants had dug in the days of Abraham his father, and they had filled them with earth" (Gen. 26:15). These were Abraham's wells, and Isaac was going to re-dig the wells of his father.

The Church must remember to honor our spiritual fathers. Christians of the past, like John Wesley, Martin Luther, and other spiritual fathers, had breakthroughs, and we now enjoy the advantage of their breakthroughs. They have already broken spiritual ground with certain truths that had not previously been released. Now we can hold on to the revelation the Lord gave them and build upon it.

We must remember that we are in times of restoration. There have been a lot of things restored over the last ten years, but the Lord is bringing us into our fruitfulness, bringing us into our land. Deuteronomy 29:29a says that, *"The secret things belong to the Lord our God, but those things which are revealed belong to us and to our children forever."* Any past Kingdom breakthroughs should also be our breakthroughs. The wells of people like Kathryn Kuhlman, Smith Wigglesworth, and others are beginning to bubble up again. Any nugget of truth that was revealed in the past should be enjoyed by us today and by our children through all generations. Jesus promised that He will restore all things to the Church (see Acts 3:21); and every time there is a restoration, we can walk in it. Past breakthroughs as well as current breakthroughs are for today.

I believe that we are a generation that will walk in the fullness of the Holy Spirit! The fullness makes the impossible possible for every believer. The Lord will bring it all together; and we will look not just at what used to be, or what is still coming, but we will walk in it all in the now. Remember, Jesus is the past, the present, and the future—all at the same time. This blows my mind!

So, we need to honor our spiritual fathers, and benefit from and their revelation. Isaac said, "I'm going to honor Abraham, and I'm going to take back his wells that the Philistines (*Philistine* represents satan) have filled with dirt." *Earth* or *dirt* stands for man. The enemy uses men to plug the wells. The traditions of man and religion put different names on the wells of revival of the past, which just plug them up and make them useless.

Isaac re-dug the wells that the enemy had covered up, got them flowing again, and reinstated their original names. But he didn't stop there. He dug three new wells.

STIRRING OF HUNGER

We have enjoyed 12 or 13 years of renewal, which is awesome, but I feel the Lord is saying, "There's much more for you right now." The Word says we go from glory to glory! (See Second Corinthians 3:18.) So how does the Lord open up these wells? He begins by initiating *holy hunger* in His people's hearts to see the wells restored. Haggai 1:14 says that God stirred up the spirit of the remnant. He arouses us in our inner man, or awakens our hearts. So we begin calling out to the Lord for the very thing He has awakened us to receive.

The Lord begins to awaken His people to the wells (moves of God) from the past. All through the Bible spiritual leaders ask, "Remember the God of your fathers who parted the Red Sea;

remember the great and mighty things He did in your midst?" He begins to stir up the people by way of recalling His deeds of the past, and that causes us to begin to be hungry and dissatisfied with our present situation. We begin to *cry out to Him in prayer*, and that's what starts the re-digging of the wells. The Lord wants us to *re-dig the wells* of the fathers to honor them, but this time they'll never be plugged up again. Do you know why? The Lord told me this. Because the wells are beginning to bubble now, and the ones who begin to partake of that living water will become ones who don't hold it for themselves. They will become distributors of the water, rivers of living water; they will help establish these truths in the Church once again. There will be thousands and thousands who will move and operate out of that dimension, and the enemy can never stop its flow again, because there will just be too many people doing it! Jesus is the "was" (the wells of the old), and He wants us to re-dig these wells so they flow freely; He wants those lost aspects of the Kingdom to be present again in the Church.

A few months ago the Lord told me, "The ears of the masses have grown dull."

I said, "Well, what's it going to take to open them?"

"Power preaching," He said.

It was said of John Wesley's meetings that people would tell others, "Don't get in the trees." When Wesley opened his mouth, the power of the Holy Spirit began to flow, and people would fall.

One thing that the Lord is going to do is put in people's hands the "sword of the Lord" (see Heb. 4:12) that cuts through and removes everything that is not of God. People like this have broken through in certain realms in the Kingdom, just like Isaac broke through the old wells.

We could say that a mantle is a well. A mantle never returns to the Lord until it fulfills the commissioning of God. I am totally convinced that the Lord has commissioned a breakthrough to be established in the Church on a daily basis in believers' lives.

EXAMPLE OF ELIJAH AND ELISHA

The call of the prophet Elisha exemplifies this progression of hunger followed by pursuit and breakthrough. (See First Kings 19.) Before God called him to be a prophet, Elisha had his own plans. He was minding his own business, plowing the field with his "Cadillac" oxen and cart, when along came the prophet Elijah. Elijah took his mantle and went *bam!* Elisha probably thought, *What was that?* But such a hunger for God gripped Elisha that he said, "Forget the oxen, forget the field, I'm going after this mantle!"

Before I got saved my goal was to have the biggest electrical business and a big home in Texas. But God had something more in mind for my life.

You also have a vision that God has put in your heart; you've tasted something in the Spirit, and you are being stirred to pursue Him. Press into God! He is not like the world, which dangles an unattainable carrot in front of you. Do you know that what God reveals to you, He wants to give to you?

Elisha pursued Elijah, and the day came when he got a new commissioning from the Lord. Elisha picked up Elijah's mantle, and he said, "*Where is the Lord God of Elijah?*" (See Second Kings 2:9-14.) Elisha went out and did double what Elijah had done. The Lord is doing the same thing in the Body of Christ right now. He's releasing scrolls, books of destiny, that He wants us to eat, and receive into our spirits (see Ezek. 3:1-2). This is the season we are in right now.

There's an anointing for restoration of the desolate heritages right now. In fact, God is going to favor some apostolic centers to begin to actually bring restoration and rebuild the desolation of generations. In other words, the wells of the old, the wells of the now, and the wells to come are all starting to flow together in fullness. Do you want the fullness of the Spirit? When Elisha received the mantle of Elijah, he began to operate in that anointing.

THE WELL OF THE SEVEN

In this present restoration time, we are going to begin to see some of these anointings be restored to the Church. We are not supposed to make our ministries look like their ministries, but we are supposed to move in the power that they moved in.

Isaac re-dug three wells of the old, and then dug three new ones, the wells of the now. There's one more well I want to talk about.

Genesis 26:33 reveals that God gave Isaac one last well to dig, the best one of all, the icing on the proverbial cake. Its name was *Shebah* (or Shibah), meaning "the well of the seven." How would you like to drink from all seven wells? That is the fullness of God. That is the manifold blessings of the Holy Spirit, the seven Spirits of God.

This same well still stands today and provides fresh pure water to the thirsty. It still beckons the thirsty because it sustains, satisfies, and fulfills.

We're not to settle with only the past, present, or future wells, but the fullness of all of them. Why don't you put your hand on your belly right now and just say, "Shebah, fullness!" Ask the Lord for His very best.

BUILDING BY THE SEVEN

The Spirit of the Lord shall rest upon Him, the spirit of wisdom and understanding, the spirit of counsel and might, and the spirit of knowledge and of the fear of the Lord. His delight is in the fear of the Lord, and He shall not judge by the sight of His eyes, nor decide by the hearing of His ears; but with righteousness He shall judge the poor, and decide with equity for the meek of the earth; He shall strike the earth with the rod of His mouth, and with the breath of His lips He shall slay the wicked. Righteousness shall be the belt of His loins, and faithfulness the belt of His waist (Isaiah 11:2-5).

When the Church starts moving in the fullness of these seven spirits of God as Jesus did, we'll see the results shown in this passage. The Lord wants to release the Church into this realm of the fullness of God where we begin to implement justice and righteousness upon the earth by the power of the Holy Spirit.

What is injustice? It is anything that is not of the Kingdom of God. And the Church will begin to minister in a manner like what Jesus explained in John 5:19, "*I say to you, the Son can do nothing of Himself, but what He sees the Father do; for whatever He does, the Son also does in like manner.*"

When the Church begins to move and operate out of this dimension, we will no longer judge by hearsay or our natural senses. We will begin to move in the counsel of Heaven and begin to implement justice and righteousness. We want justice for every injustice the devil has performed, and we'll ask and see the Lord bring godly justice. We will not do it by our own motives, but by hearing and seeing from the Spirit.

The weight of our words will carry great power as we move in this realm. God is raising up a "Samuel generation" with weighty words that will not fall to the ground (see 1 Sam. 3:19). Their words will never return void as they operate in this realm of open heavens, or fullness.

One of the effects of this kind of outpouring is Isaiah 32:15-17. It says,

> *Until the Spirit is poured upon us from on high, and the wilderness becomes a fruitful field, and the fruitful field is counted as a forest. Then justice will dwell in the wilderness, and righteousness remain in the fruitful field. The work of righteousness will be peace, and the effect of righteousness, quietness and assurance forever.*

Wouldn't you like to live in peace, quietness, and a security in your inner self? In the realm of Kingdom dominion you are not tossed to and fro, but you are very strong in the stature of Christ. By His divine power, you become a partaker of His divine nature (see 2 Peter 1:4). The Church will begin to see the effects of injustice being made right, verdicts being rendered back to those who have been beaten, stolen from, and robbed by satan. Justice will roll down like a river as the seven flows gush through the government of Jesus in His Church!

THE SEVEN IS UNLIMITED ANOINTING

After Jesus' resurrection, all the disciples were assembled together in a room, and guess who walked through the wall (He didn't knock on the door)? I imagine their hair stood straight up! He said, "Peace." But the next thing He said to them was an incredible statement: "*As the Father has sent Me, I also send you*" (John 20:21). When Jesus made that statement, He was sending them out in His own anointing, which is described in John 3:34: *"For He whom God has sent speaks the words of God, for God does not give the Spirit by measure."*

Have you ever experienced the anointing without measure? I haven't yet, but I want to see it! What does it look like? Just look at Jesus! He lived in the anointing without measure. When Heaven opened at Jesus' baptism, the Holy Spirit came and rested on Him in the fullness, or without measure (see Mark 1:10). And Jesus said, "I'm going to send you out the same way the Father sent Me." I believe we're the generation that will see the Holy Spirit "without measure." Jesus even said in John 14:12, *"Most assuredly, I say to you, he who believes in Me, the works that I do he will do also; and **greater works** than these he will do, because I go to My Father."* This is so amazing!

So the Lord is setting the stage for a people who will walk in the Spirit without measure through the fullness of the seven Spirits of God. When we do, the world will begin to marvel at the wisdom and power of the Church, because we will begin to look just like Jesus as we operate in His anointing.

CHAPTER 8

The Spirit of God Upon

T HE first flow of the sevenfold expression of the Holy Spirit described in Isaiah 11:2 *"the Spirit of the Lord shall rest upon Him,"* is *communion with the Lord Himself.* This is the place of intimacy with Him that releases all the other six expressions of the Holy Spirit in and through your life.

I love this because the word rest here means "to settle upon; to come upon; to rest upon; to settle down and remain." This same word is used in Isaiah 61:1, *"The Spirit of the Lord God is upon Me, because the Lord has anointed Me to preach good tidings to the poor...."* I believe this "resting upon" is a *crowning.* He decides to set that crown of His tangible, or manifested, presence upon you. Kathryn Kuhlman moved and operated in the "Spirit of the Lord upon." Pastor Benny Hinn does as well. I believe that God intends any believer who so desires to walk in the place of deep communion with the Spirit of the Lord upon their life. I also like to call this "the secret place" of the presence of God, as mentioned in Psalm 91:1, *"He who dwells in the secret place of the Most High shall abide under the shadow of the Almighty."* If the Spirit is resting upon you, you are living under His shadow. How awesome is that?

A couple of years back in one of our meetings, I was just coming into the flow of the Holy Spirit in a certain way. I was sitting on the platform, when a lady came up to me and said, "I want what's on you." I thought, *What?* I didn't understand. At that point, I had been pressing in for the things the Lord had been showing me, and I had been *spending a considerable amount of time in His presence*. I actually had a tangible, manifest presence of God *upon* me. She could actually see it! The Spirit upon is tangible! I believe that each and every one of us ought to come out of our prayer closets looking, smelling, and being a little bit different, don't you? Wouldn't you like the Spirit of God to come and rest upon you? This isn't questioning if the Spirit of God is in you, but it is a mantle that rests upon your life as well.

ABIDING IN THE VINE

Isaiah 11:1 says, "*There shall come forth a Rod from the stem of Jesse, and a Branch shall grow out of his roots.*" Now this is important. Where did the branch come from? John 15:5 says you will be fruitful by abiding in Jesus: "*I am the vine, you are the branches. He who abides in Me, and I in him, bears much fruit; for without Me you can do nothing.*"

Do you want to abide in the vine? You cannot operate out of the sevenfold flow without being in Jesus the vine. This flow is mentioned first, because it is essential for all the functions of the Spirit. Everything flows out of Christ, the anointed One, and His anointing. As we have already seen from Second Peter 1:3-4, you can be a partaker of His divine nature by the Spirit of the Lord who *is* the main Branch. It is your inheritance to be plugged into the Branch of Christ Jesus:

> *If the firstfruit is holy, the lump is also holy; and if the root is holy, so are the branches. And if some of the branches were broken off, and you, being a wild olive tree, were grafted in among them, and with them*

become a partaker of the root and the fatness of the olive tree" (Romans 11:16-17).

So we become a partaker of the root. Who is the root? The Lord is the branch and He's the Root, the Alpha and the Omega. And the *fatness* here means the richness, the fresh flourishing oil to live in that capacity. Everything flows out of the manifest presence. All seven functions have to flow out of the Lord's presence.

Abiding means "locking in, or engaging in union with Christ." Where is Christ? If you are a Christian, He is in you. Union with Him means *engaging*. Engaging is like two gears locked together; they come together as one but they are still separate. Union with Christ is a spirit-to-Spirit engaging. The Scripture says that *"you being a wild olive tree,"* with "wild" meaning lost.

Before I was saved, I was wild; you may have been wild as well. But a wonderful thing took place; the moment you were saved, you were grafted into the olive tree. You were grafted *to the root.* The root supplies nourishment to the branches. We want the character of God to be flowing into our lives. His character is holiness, His nature is love, and His Power is unlimited. Thus we can see His attributes through our lives, because we are part of His tree.

Being grafted into the olive tree will also release in our lives the fruit of the Spirit—*"love, joy, peace, longsuffering, kindness, goodness, faithfulness, gentleness, self-control"* (Gal. 5:22-23). We see each of these in the Master's life. As we are ministering in this abiding anointing, we will see the sevenfold Holy Spirit expression through our lives daily, but we will also see an abundance of the fruit of the Spirit released. It is not about performance; it is all about *abiding.* We express what we are partaking of through our lives.

In Psalm 92:10, the word *"anointed with fresh oil"* means the *overflow of fresh oil.* Living from His presence upon you and through you proclaims to others that you are anointed with His presence.

You read in previous chapters that the Holy Spirit came upon Jesus in the fullness, or without measure. We can see that the Holy Spirit *rested upon or remained on* Him like a dove at His baptism. He moved in a constant presence and abiding of the fullness of the Holy Spirit. He received without measure every aspect of the person, ministry, and expression of all that the wonderful Holy Spirit is. This is the very essence of abiding in Him. The abiding presence of the Holy Spirit is the Spirit of the Lord upon. We cannot see any of the expressions, functions, fruit, gifts, or manifestations of the Holy Spirit without the river of His glorious presence.

THE CENTER PIPE

I make mention of many things repeatedly in this book for emphasis, one being the passage in Zechariah 4:1-14. Read it several times and study it. It uses a picture of a golden or lampstand with seven oil lamps on top of it to show a clear and visible picture of the seven flows of the Holy Spirit. To paraphrase, the angel said to Zechariah, "Look here, you are going to see something that is going to release the perpetual, ceaseless supply of the Holy Spirit; where your hands will be dripping with oil, and you will be called sons of fresh anointing." The vision included the lampstand, because it shows first the center pipe with the vat and the two olive trees. I believe the two olive trees are the Word and the Spirit. I want to live in both the living Word and the fresh anointing of the Lord.

The *center pipe is Christ*, the mediator between us and God. The six flows (tubes) plus one in the middle equal *seven*, the number of fullness. *You cannot have the fullness without being tapped into the center pipe*, Jesus. From the middle of the lamp-stand, three pairs of pipes go outward on opposite sides. The three pairs represent the three pairings of flows in Isaiah 11:2: *"wisdom and understanding...counsel and might...knowledge and...the fear of the Lord."*

THE GLORY OF THE LATTER HOUSE
WILL BE GREATER

I believe God is calling people to learn how to make their abode or stay in what Jesus paid the way for them to receive, to make the throne room their habitation. I believe we are in the hour when we can begin to believe for the Lord to release this measure of the mantles of the characteristics of the seven Spirits of God operating through our lives, through churches, cities, and regions. Why do you think the Lord comes and sits upon a person, a church, or even a nation? Over the years we have seen how the Lord shows up in manifest presence, and history is made. I once heard a man say that if you took a little piece of land anywhere in the world, and the Spirit of the Lord came upon that place, people would flock from around world to that place because of His manifest presence.

When Jesus went to the Mount of Transfiguration, the glory of God came upon Him and He *radiated brilliancy*. I believe we will see this holy glow again!

When Moses came down from being with God on the mountain, his face was literally glowing (see Exod. 34:29). Moses said something awesome to the Lord. *"For how then will it be known that Your people and I have found grace in Your sight, except You go with us? So we shall be separate, Your people and I, from all the people who are upon the face of the earth"* (Exod. 33:16). He had been in the presence of the Lord. Moses is a forerunner for the whole Body of Christ, and the Bible says that the glory of the latter house will be even greater than that of Moses! (See Second Corinthians 3:7-18; Haggai 2:9 KJV.)

> *Arise shine; for your light has come! And the glory of the Lord is risen upon you. For behold, the darkness shall cover the earth, and deep darkness the people; but the Lord will arise over you, and His glory will be seen upon you. The Gentiles shall come to your light, and kings to the brightness of your rising* (Isaiah 60:1-3).

One time our ministry went to Cedar Rapids, Iowa City, and Fairfield, Iowa. I could not believe the realm of anointing that was released in the meetings! I actually felt and saw the *swirlings* of God during this time! We had to stop the meetings because the Holy Spirit was moving so powerfully as I walked through the crowds of the people to minister the Holy Spirit was moving in such power that 10, 15, even 20 people at a time was literally being over come and falling into the metal chairs and on to the concrete. I was thinking, *Man, somebody is going to get hurt.* We were in the mighty flow of the Holy Spirit, or the river of His manifest presence. I can always tell when the shift takes place. I begin ministering in the gift, but all of a sudden it shifts into the flow of the river of His presence.

Several years ago I heard a story about a camp meeting where, right in the midst of praise and worship, five fire trucks pulled up to the tent with their sirens going. Everyone under the tent came running out asking, "What's going on?"

One of the firemen said, "Your tent is on fire!" The entire top of the tent was glowing! There was no fire, but it was the manifest, tangible presence of God settling upon the tent.

Maria Woodworth-Etter (1844–1924) was used by God in such a mighty way that hundreds of thousands of souls were saved, and millions of lives were charged and changed through her ministry and writings. When she set up a revival tent in town, the power of God would hit people for 25 miles around. She carried a huge mantle of the manifest presence of the Spirit of God upon.

It is time to get past timidness and press in violently to God for this. In meetings like Benny Hinn's, I have watched people push other people out of the way, just to get the impartation of the Spirit. (I won't mention any names.) I believe we should have that same type of hunger for the Spirit for our lives. Only arrogance and pride keep us from being desperate for Him. But these attitudes are coming down.

There is a story about the ministry of Smith Wigglesworth. One time when he was on a train, everyone in the car he was riding in was saved! It is said that when Kathryn Kuhlman would walk into a building, the chefs in the kitchen would get touched by the power of God. Have you ever been in a meeting, and when somebody walked in you thought, *That person is carrying something?* The *something* is the Spirit of God resting upon. Raise your hands to the Lord right now and say, "Lord, I want that. Come, Holy Spirit. Rest upon me. Amen."

PETER RECEIVED THE SPIRIT UPON

I want to show you one other thing from the Scripture that is blessing me big time, and I hope that it will encourage you and stir you up to press in for all that Jesus has for you! The disciples had postured themselves according to the word that Jesus gave them in Luke 24:49 about receiving the power from on high. Acts 2:1 says, "*When the day of Pentecost had fully come, they were all in one accord in one place.*" Their hearts were in line with Heaven. Their hearts' cry was, "We want Your heart and mind, Lord. We want what You promised us, Lord. Here we are, hungry after You. We don't know what this is going to look like, and we really don't care. We just know that we are calling out to *You!*"

Notice it said that when Pentecost had "fully come." It was what He had purposed to do. Others were invited, but only these came. But He purposed to release the promise upon the earth at the fullness of time. It was the place in time that He marked and chose!

The visitation of the Holy Spirit described in the beginning of Acts 2, brought these disciples a life-changing encounter. Something beyond them had taken place. Once they were one way, and now they were another. Three thousand people were born again in one day (Acts 2:41), many were healed, and sign and wonders were taking place in such magnitude that the city was gripped with the fear of the Lord (Acts 2:43). We need to see that in our cities!

One day John and Peter were on their way to temple prayers when they met a crippled man. Looking at him, Peter said, "*Silver and gold I do not have, but what I do have I give you: In the name of Jesus Christ of Nazareth, rise up and walk*" (Acts 3:6). Peter extended his hand to the man, who began leaping and praising the Lord. Wow! Even those who had opposed the disciples called that healing a notable miracle (Acts 4:13-16).

After their arrest and release, Peter and John rejoined the other disciples and told what had happened. The group immediately began to pray, reminding God that in the past, their enemies had conspired against Jesus "*to do whatever Your hand and Your purpose determined before to be done*" (Acts 4:27b). They plugged into the Word and the Spirit! They were saying, "Even with threats against us, we want the living Word and the anointing! We want to see an even greater release of the hand of God through our lives; we want to heal and do signs and wonders through Jesus." Then, "*the place where they were assembled together was shaken; and they were all filled with the Holy*

Spirit, and they spoke the word of God with boldness" (Acts 4:31). Then they received great power and great grace!

All of a sudden Peter's ministry completely changed. In Acts 3:7, we see him ministering to *one* person, out of the *gift* of the Holy Spirit. But now the Holy Spirit was flowing like a river. In Acts 5:15-16 we see Peter walking in such an open heaven that the tangible presence of the Holy Spirit poured out of Peter. People just wanted to touch him, or even cloths that he had prayed over. He moved from flowing in the gift to flowing in the rivers. He went from gift to open heavens. He went from one to multitudes! The river of the Spirit of God upon his life was uncapped.

I find it interesting that, having experienced these open heavens, Peter wrote:

> *His divine power has given to us all things* [I love the word *all*] *that pertain to life and godliness, through the knowledge of Him who called us by glory and virtue, by which have been given to us exceedingly great and precious promises, that through these you may be partakers of the divine nature* (2 Peter 1:3-4a).

You've got to understand that what you have been going through in your Christian walk is bringing you into union with Christ. It becomes not I who live, but He who lives in me (see Gal. 2:20).

Peter went on to say, "*But also for this very reason, giving all diligence, add to your faith virtue, to virtue knowledge, to knowledge self-control, to self-control perseverance, to perseverance godliness, to godliness brotherly kindness, and to brotherly kindness love*" (2 Pet. 1:5-7). In other words, he said, "I'm always contending; contending; contending." Do you know why? It is because God is concerned about our character. God wants to reveal His glory through our lives. It doesn't mean just a touch of glory. No, the glory is *Him*. It is *His presence*. It is who He is; the weightiness of God. He wants to demonstrate glory through as you come into union with Christ's character, His nature, and His power—by the enabling of the Holy Spirit. This is not just a suggestion from your spouse; this is *God*.

It is all worth it! All the pressure, all the hammering, all the change, all the transition, and all the internal things that are taking place within you are worth it. Embrace it all, because He is worth it. Benny Hinn and Reinhard Bonnke have a mandate, but you have one too. Say to yourself, "I have a mandate too. He wants to manifest in my life *as it is in heaven upon the earth*. He wants to demonstrate His nature, His character, and His power through His Spirit upon me." If, as he sat in the garden after denying Christ three times, Peter had heard about his future—open heavens, etc.—he would have said, "No way!" Your lowest moment should be when you press in the most!

I want to encourage you that you are going to become a daily partaker of His very divine nature in you, just like Peter eventually did. He wrote, "*For so an entrance will be supplied* [continuously supplied] *to you abundantly into the everlasting Kingdom of our Lord and Savior Jesus Christ*" (2 Pet. 1:11). In other words, the Lord wants to give you a place where you begin to operate out of a continuous manifestation of the realm of the Kingdom. Do you want that kind of realm? Ask for the Spirit of the Lord to rest upon you like Peter did. He wants to do this even more than you know! It was His idea and desire to take up residence in humanity. And it was His sovereign will before the foundation of the world to take up residency in you. Isn't that tremendous?

CHAPTER 9

The Spirit of Wisdom, Part One

As you have read, Isaiah 11:2 speaks of the seven Spirits of God. There is only one Holy Spirit, but seven different functions—anointings, expressions, or flows—of the Holy Spirit. The first of the seven, the *Spirit of the Lord resting upon*, is the *anointing of His manifest presence*. Revelation 3:1 says that *Jesus* has the seven Spirits of God, and in Revelation 1:4 we see that the seven Spirits of God are before His throne.

After I had the visitation from the angel who handed me an envelope bearing the references *Revelation 4:5* and *Isaiah 11:2*, I began researching the seven Spirits of God. The Lord impressed upon me that while it was important to *preach* about the seven Spirits of God, I should also *live* in the full operation of His sevenfold flow. As the Lord began to show me different aspects about the seven Spirits, I started praying, "Well, let it be done unto me according to that flow."

Several years ago the Lord taught me about the *Spirit of wisdom* in a manner that my wife, Janet, and I will never forget! As I was ministering in Winnie, Texas, I had a "Maria Woodworth-Etter experience." While preaching, I suddenly froze and went into a trance. It was the most incredible thing. (Of course, I say that about everything the Lord does.)

I saw the Lord speak a word, and I saw the word come into me and expand into a paragraph. The paragraph became several paragraphs, turned into books—and then book after book started coming into me.

When I came out of this trance experience, my wife said "I want that too. I know something just happened to you; I can tell and I want it." After this Holy Ghost download, the *Spirit of wisdom* began to operate in my life.

CHAPTER OVERVIEW

In this chapter I will explain from the Bible:

- Definition.

- Function.

- Benefit.

- Transfer of the anointing.

In the following chapter, also dealing with the Spirit of wisdom, I will give Old and New Testament examples, and also some amazing, recent-day testimonies of the spirit of wisdom at work.

SPIRIT OF WISDOM DEFINED

The Spirit of wisdom is not just information. The Spirit of wisdom is a *supernatural endowment of an ability to do something above one's own ability*. It is actually *the skillful ability to do what God has called you to do*. There is a river of wisdom being released to the Church right now—not analytical ability, but a skillful and *creative ability*. Psalm 136:5a says of God, "[He] *who by wisdom made the heavens*."

The Church is about to minister out of wisdom that is going to confound the wisest people on the earth. The world will begin to ask, "Where did he get that ability? He didn't go to school for that!" Believers say, "I got it in a dream." People will be mystified by this.

Benny Hinn describes it like this, "Wisdom is living skills; it is the ability to apply the knowledge of God's Word to our lives daily. It involves the application of God's truth to human experience on a day-to-day basis. Properly mastered, it can lead to a happy, successful, and prosperous life." Welcome, Holy Spirit!

The Spirit of wisdom flows from Heaven, straight from His throne; it comes *out of communion with the Lord in intimacy with Him*. It flows from *His presence*, the "center pipe" of the lampstand in Zechariah 4:2, from which the other six operations of the Spirits also flow.

GIFT OF WISDOM VERSUS SPIRIT OF WISDOM

There is a distinct difference between the gift of wisdom and the Spirit of wisdom. In First Corinthians 12:8, we see the gift of wisdom, or a word of wisdom: "*for to one is given the word of wisdom through the Spirit, to another the word of knowledge through the same Spirit.*" We give words of wisdom when the Holy Spirit uses us to deliver a particular piece of information— possibly about a healing, a wayward child, etc.

The Lord wants us to take it up a notch and experience the continuous flow of the Spirit of wisdom. He is moving us into the function of the Holy Spirit where we will walk in the perpetual, ceaseless flow of the unlimited anointing, not just every once in a while. So we want more than just a word of wisdom, we want a river of wisdom; we want the Spirit of wisdom.

FUNCTION OF SPIRIT OF WISDOM

John 7:38b says, "*Out of his* [your] *heart* [belly] *will flow rivers of living water.*" These rivers symbolize multiple flows or functions of the Holy Spirit. Think about the *Spirit of wisdom* as a river of wisdom flowing out of your life. As was stated earlier, wisdom is not analytical ability, but *creative power*. So the Spirit of wisdom is an impartation or a river of *creative ability to function in what God is calling you to do*.

As I write this, I am feeling the zeal of the Holy Spirit very strongly.

Rivers represent several different expressions or functions of the Holy Spirit ministry. One of those flows is the Spirit of wisdom. So, as a believer you have the potential to have a river of wisdom flow *from* you, *through* you, and *around* you, as Ephesians 1:19 suggests.

Jesus is wise, is He not? He sees the beginning from the end and the end from the beginning. He is the Alpha and Omega. He has the blueprint for your life right in front of Him. He has what God has already ordained for you. He hears from the Father, "Jesus, go get it," and then He tells the Holy Spirit, who transmits it to you.

I believe that my potential in any area is unlimited. It is not based on how well I can do things, but on how I learn to flow with the river of wisdom. Since He gives me supernatural ability to do things, I want to cause people who have not seen me in three years say, "Oh, my, look at this guy! Where's he getting this stuff from?" And I can give the Lord glory for it all.

People said of Jesus, "*Where did this Man get these things? And what wisdom is this which is given to Him, that such mighty works are performed by His hands!*" (Mark 6:2b). You see, we need that again in the Church. We need to set the standard for the world.

BENEFITS OF THE SPIRIT OF WISDOM

Look at this passage, which is all about wisdom:

Get wisdom! Get understanding! Do not forget, nor turn away from the words of my mouth. Do not forsake her, and she will preserve you; love her, and she will keep you. Wisdom is the principal thing; therefore get wisdom. And in all your getting, get understanding. Exalt her, and she will promote you; she will bring you honor, when you embrace her. She will place on your head an ornament of grace; a crown of glory she will deliver to you. Hear, my son, and receive my sayings, and the years of your life will be many. I have taught you in the way of wisdom; I have led you in right paths. When you walk, your steps will not be hindered, and when you run, you will not stumble. Take firm hold of instruction, do not let go; keep her, for she is your life (Proverbs 4:5-13).

PROMOTION

The Spirit of wisdom will bring promotion. Grace is *favor, or supernatural ability to do what you can't do*; He does it for you.

I have always had this kind of favor. I have wondered, *Why do I always get these breaks?* I used to call it luck.

Once a man told me, "By the way, I am going to give you a racehorse."

I said, "I don't need a racehorse."

He said, "Oh, you don't have to do anything."

I said, "Well, how much does it cost to feed that thing?"

He said, "No, I'll feed it too. I just want to put your name on it."

I asked, "Why?"

He said, "Everything you touch turns to gold."

It was because of God's *favor*. I believe the Lord allowed me to touch that side of life because I came from such a bad background. We were very poor. When I was young, I stole clothes off people's clotheslines to help my brothers and sisters. Can you imagine going to school and being asked, "Hey, isn't that my shirt?" It's kind of embarrassing. I used to go to the grocery store at 4 a.m. to steal the food that was set outside the store for stock. I knew that side of life. The Lord's goodness allowed me to know His favor, and that is what is so awesome about His plan. He later allowed me to prosper in business, an advantage that reaped not only finances, but also important life lessons. Riches do not entice me anymore. I have already had them and I was still empty. Wealth cannot compare to what I have now. I would never trade the anointing for any amount of money!

LONG LIFE

Did you know that wisdom will extend your life? The Lord once told me, "Keith, a lot of My people are dying prematurely due to stress. If they would just embrace the Spirit of wisdom, they would have a lot less stress." Proverbs 4:10 says, "*Hear, my son, and receive my sayings, and the years of your life will be many."* When people try to live by their own abilities instead of plugging into His ability, stress increases.

God has purposes and plans for every believer. His plans are bigger than what you can do. They will either drive you or excite you. We usually go through a season when we are driven by our vision—when we get worn out, weary, and give up, God kicks in and begins to do it through us.

We do not have to live driven, weary lives! We can actually live in His wisdom. Jesus said, *"Take My yoke upon you.... For My yoke is easy and My burden is light"* (Matt. 11:29-30).

AN ORNAMENT OF GRACE

"Wisdom will place on your head an ornament of grace and crown your head with glory." God says, "Let Me put an ornament of grace on your head." Everywhere you go, that ornament is there. Rejoice, because grace gives you favor with God and man. Grace gives you what you do not deserve. Grace makes things easy. *"You therefore, my son, be strong in the grace that is in Christ Jesus"* (2 Tim. 2:1). The word *strong* means to be enabled or energized by grace. When we operate out of the function of wisdom, we are energized by grace, not by our strength.

We will find many things to be hard when we try to operate out of natural wisdom instead of the Spirit of wisdom. We wonder why the Lord is not glorified when we struggle and finally get it done. I am tired of what we can do. I want to see some things that only God can do.

The Spirit of wisdom and understanding will promote you, put an ornament of glory over your head, and then crown you with glory. We read that Moses had to put a veil over his face because of the glory. When God crowns you with glory, you become more God-conscious than self- or sin-conscious. What changes might occur in your life if you became crowned with glory, the weightiness of His character, His nature and His power?

PEACE

*Happy is the man who finds wisdom, and the man who gains understanding; for her proceeds are better than the profits of silver, her gain than fine gold. She is more precious than rubies, and all the things you may desire cannot compare with her. Length of days is in her right hand, in her left hand, riches and honor. Her ways are ways of pleasantness, and **all of her paths are peace**. She is a tree of life to those who take hold of her, and happy are all who retain her. The Lord by wisdom founded the earth; by understanding He established the heavens; by His knowledge the depths were broken up, and clouds drop down the dew* (Proverbs 3:13-20).

Christians should be at peace, knowing that what He asks of us, He is not asking us to do in our own ability. He will give you the Spirit of wisdom to perform the very thing He is asking of you. When you begin to minister out of the Spirit of wisdom, you won't be in a state of emotional reaction; you will be at peace.

Jesus operated in a constant flow of the Spirit of wisdom. His works, words, and teachings astonished the multitudes. Jesus provided the disciples with a great supply of opportunities to marvel. He commanded the fig tree to wither (Matt. 21:19-20), calmed a raging sea with a word (Mark 6:51), and boldly declared to the skeptical Pharisees and Herodians, "*Render to Caesar the things that are Caesar's, and to God the things that are God's*"

(Mark 12:17).All who heard Him were astonished with His teaching, (Luke 4:32), His understanding, and His answers (Luke 2:47). He did many wonderful things, even raised the dead. It doesn't get much more astonishing than that!

In Acts 6:10 we read of Stephen, "*And they were not able to resist the wisdom and the Spirit by which he spoke.*" This is incredible manifestation of the Spirit of wisdom through a person. Jesus said, "*I will give you a mouth and wisdom which all your adversaries will not be able to contradict or resist*" (Luke 21:15). This is functioning out of the Spirit of wisdom rather than an emotional response. This is a place of the peace of God Ruling and Reigning in you. You respond out of the place of wisdom. As a believer the Lord wants you to be able to speak life to the hurting and lead many to Christ. "*The Lord God has given Me the tongue of the learned, that I should know how to speak a word in season to him who is weary. He awakens Me morning by morning, He awakens My ear to hear as the learned*" (Isaiah 50:4).

Many people will be led to Christ through the operation of the Spirit of wisdom. Daniel 12:3 says, "*Those who are wise shall shine like the brightness of the firmament, and those who turn many to righteousness like the stars forever and ever.*" What a powerful tool!

CLEVER LIVING

God's people should be the wittiest people on the earth; we should be the ones who set the standard. Instead, we seem to always make excuses such as, "Well, if I had what they had…" The truth is—you do have the advantage over unbelievers. You have the Holy Spirit living in you. Jesus Himself said, "It's to your advantage that I go away so He [the Holy Spirit] can come" (see John 16:7).

One of my favorite Scriptures is Nehemiah 9:20a, "*You also gave Your good Spirit to instruct them.*" God has given us His best, and the word for *best* means "beautiful, bountiful." The Holy Spirit is His best one who can *instruct* us. The word instruct means "to shoot like an arrow; to guide wittily, like a wise master builder." Christians should be the ones operating in the most skillful realms of ability and wisdom, because we are plugged into the One who is orchestrating and bringing forth everything that He has purposed since the foundations of the earth.

Living your life wittily will make people around you take notice. God wants to do something in our lives that gives Him glory. Do not limit yourself to your education and your natural ability. I believe with all of my heart that the Spirit of wisdom is for every believer; it doesn't matter whether you are 7 or 70.

HEAVENLY BLUEPRINTS—GOD'S PLANS FOR US

You can begin to operate daily in the river of wisdom. Courses of action from God will enable you to be a wise master builder, following custom-made heavenly blueprints just for you. God has rivers of wisdom available to us for our lives. He has ordained our days before they ever come to pass.

> *I will praise You, for I am fearfully and wonderfully made; marvelous are Your works, and that my soul knows very well. My frame was not hidden from You, when I was made in secret, and skillfully wrought in the lowest parts of the earth. Your eyes saw my substance, being yet unformed. And in Your book they all were written, the days fashioned for*

me, when as yet there were none of them. How pre-
cious also are Your thoughts to me, O God! How great
is the sum of them! If I should count them, they
would be more in number than the sand; when I
awake, I am still with You (Psalm 139:14-18).

I love the thought that my days are fashioned for me in the
Lord's book in advance!

For we are His workmanship, created in Christ Jesus
for good works, which God prepared beforehand that
we should walk in them (Ephesians 2:10).

No longer do I call you servants, for a servant does not
know what his master is doing; but I have called you
friends, for all things that I heard from My Father I have
made known to you. You did not choose Me, but I chose
you and appointed you that you should go and bear fruit,
and that your fruit should remain, that whatever you ask
the Father in My name He may give you (John 15:15-16).

Do you want the fruit in your life that He has ordained and
prepared? Do you want wisdom in order to walk out His eternal
blueprint? A river of wisdom will bring them about. Wisdom is
more important than any riches of this earth, as Proverbs 8:11
says: *"For wisdom is better than rubies, and all the things one*
may desire cannot be compared with her."

SPIRIT OF WISDOM IMPARTATION
IS TRANSFERABLE

I preached this message in a church in Austin, Texas. I told
them, "I am going to ask the Lord to release this for you." I prayed

for the impartation and activation of the river of wisdom and understanding.

In attendance was a businessman who could hardly pay his rent. Shortly after I preached that message, he began selling a machine to refurbish computer components. Now he can't keep up with the orders. He just wrote me a check for $15,000 to build an orphanage, because the Lord is blessing him so supernaturally in the area of finances. Several other people also reported that their businesses, ministries, etc. have accelerated 20 times over. As a man believes, so shall he receive. Every believer can live in a river of the wisdom of the Holy Spirit—not just every once in a while, but daily.

The Lord wants you to enter into another level of the Spirit of wisdom. I am going to ask and believe for you to receive the activation of it. The Holy Spirit is the wisest person on the earth. He knows what is going on in Heaven. By one Spirit we have access to the Father. So, when you connect with the Spirit of wisdom or the river of wisdom, you are truly plugging in to a greater level of the wisest Person on the earth. You are going to flow with the Person who knows everything that is going on in Heaven and has access to the One who has your blueprints.

Please make these faith declarations with me aloud in *prayer*:

We are coming into sync right now with the plan of Heaven for our lives upon the earth. We are going to walk in such a realm of the Spirit that we will gain strength; we are going to increase and be fruitful because, we will operate by the Spirit of wisdom. We will build as wise master builders— not with wood, hay or stubble. We are going to build with gold and silver.

The Holy Spirit is going to search out the deep things of God and reveal them to us, then He is going to give us wisdom to implement and see the fulfillment of those things. We thank You that we are a people who are being led and instructed to live wisely and wittily by the Holy Spirit. Our steps are ordered by the Holy Spirit. Our lives will confound the wise.

This year is going to be the greatest year that we've seen for building the Kingdom, and we will be amazed at what You are going to do. Lord, because we have embraced the Spirit of wisdom, You are going to promote us. You are putting that ornament of grace on our heads right now. I thank You for the crowning of glory. I thank You, Lord, that we are going to have long life—because we are going to know a sense of rest in the Spirit that we have never known before. We are not going to do it by our strength and our ability, but by the river of wisdom.

Lord, I thank You that right now You are releasing an ability to teach like never before. I thank You, Lord, that You have given us patterns to build by. Now the Spirit of wisdom is going to see the fulfillment of those patterns. Some of those things for which we have waited ten or twenty years—this year there is going to be a thirty-, sixty-, and one hundredfold increase of them. I thank You for it all in Jesus' mighty name! Amen.

CHAPTER 10

The Spirit of Wisdom,
Part Two

WISDOM TO MAKE PRIESTLY GARMENTS

IN Exodus 28:2, the Lord told Moses to make robes for Aaron and the priests. *"You shall make holy garments for Aaron your brother, for glory and for beauty."* Did you know that robes like that had never been made before? I believe that up until that point, the priests wore plain black robes, which were not emblematic of the holiness and purity that characterized God's divine nature and the worship worthy of Him.

Moses may have asked, "How can we make garments for which there is no pattern yet?" Likely, he didn't have a clue how to proceed, because it had never been done before. The Lord answered: *"You shall speak to all who are gifted artisans, whom I have filled with the spirit of wisdom, that they may make Aaron's garments, to consecrate him, that he may minister to Me as priest"* (Exod. 28:3). No pattern existed, so they couldn't do it with their own ability. God told them to make the garments with gold, blue, purple, and scarlet thread, and gave them further intricate and detailed instructions for making them.

These artisans needed the Spirit of wisdom. The Spirit of wisdom is a *series of actions*, not analytical ability.

The Spirit of wisdom is the creative ability to function in what He is showing you. Would you like to uncap a river of the Spirit of wisdom in your life?

God is going to do what He has purposed to do. He is going to fulfill His sovereign plan. He is not a man who can lie. Do you believe that? When God releases something He wants to bring forth, He does not ask us to do it in our own ability. He releases the skills for us to operate at that level. God wants to give you the Spirit of wisdom so that you will be able to do the thing He calls you to do. He loves to call you to do the impossible, so that people around you will be astonished and say, "Where did he get this wisdom?" They said that of Jesus.

WISDOM FOR JOSHUA

Joshua loved the glory of God. Exodus 33:11 says, "*The Lord spoke to Moses face to face, as a man speaks to his friend. And he would return to the camp, but his servant Joshua the son of Nun, a young man, did not depart from the tabernacle.*" Joshua stayed in the tabernacle—he didn't want to leave the glory of God. He knew the glory, the weightiness, the character, nature, and power of God. He knew the fullness and the attributes of God. But when he knew it was time to lead the people into the Promised Land, he did not rely on just the glory.

I find it interesting that "*Joshua the son of Nun was full of the spirit of wisdom, for Moses had laid his hands on him; so the children of Israel heeded him and did as the Lord had commanded Moses*" (Deut. 34:9). He needed the Spirit of wisdom to lead the people into the Promised Land.

I believe we are coming into new seasons and new times in the Lord—new to us, not to Him. The Church needs to operate in the Spirit of wisdom and understanding now! We need to raise up a standard, not by our ability, but by being plugged into the Spirit of wisdom. This is not information or performance, but skillful ability and understanding that releases authority and strong leadership.

WISDOM FOR THE TABERNACLE OF MOSES

And He has filled him with the Spirit of God, in wisdom and understanding, in knowledge and all manner of workmanship, to design artistic works, to work in gold and silver and bronze, in cutting jewels for setting, in carving wood, and to work in all manner of artistic workmanship....in whom the Lord has put wisdom and understanding, to know how to do all manner of work for the service of the sanctuary, shall do according to all that the Lord has commanded (Exodus 35:31-33; 36:1b).

God identified for Moses the skilled craftsmen He wanted to build the tabernacle. For what God ordained them to do in the sanctuary, He would give them the Spirit of wisdom.

You need to understand that you can have the blueprint, but unless you have the wisdom and understanding, you can never implement the blueprint. He will never ask us to do anything for the Kingdom in our own ability. Worldly wisdom doesn't qualify people for His tasks. But His wisdom will confound the wisest people. The world needs to be provoked to jealousy, by the demonstration of the Spirit in power.

I do not want to just know what God has for me. I do not want to just live from prophecy to prophecy. I want to get a prophecy, or blueprint, and then see it fulfilled. Then I want to see the next one fulfilled and the one after that. Wouldn't you?

The Spirit of wisdom will do this in our lives. The Spirit of wisdom gives you ability that is beyond your ability. It is the ability to flow in the thing He is asking you to do. Wouldn't you like the Lord to uncap the rivers of Holy Spirit wisdom in your life right now and see it go from ankle to knee, knee to waist, and from waist to overflowing?

We need to build, not by the pattern of man, but by the blueprints of Heaven, where people recognize that man couldn't have done these things. Watch churches and ministries in the next few years. Some great things are going to happen; there is going to be an increase of wisdom. The Lord wants to begin to confound the wise in the world.

THE ABILITY TO TEACH

When Moses announced the craftsman God had chosen (the building contractor, in a sense), he also said that God "*has put in his heart the ability to teach*" (Exod. 35:34a).

Let's take a detour from the tabernacle design to the teaching impartation in this last verse. The Spirit of wisdom will actually give you the ability to teach. You can articulate the things in your heart God has given you. You will have clarity, because you will be speaking as an oracle of God. God can equip you to teach out of the Spirit of wisdom, to articulate in such a way that people can grasp it.

You may feel that you have something burning in you. You may have been reluctant in teaching, shy about sharing those things. You feel that you will completely mess it up if you do. But this Scripture says, "*He has put in his heart the ability to teach.*" God will do that for you too. First Peter 4:11a says, "*If anyone speaks, let him speak as the oracles of God.*"

Ask the Lord for that right now: "Lord, release the Spirit of wisdom for a teaching anointing. Let the river flow."

THE SPIRIT OF WISDOM REMOVES LIMITATIONS

Again, Exodus 36:1 says "*...and every gifted artisan in whom the Lord has put wisdom and understanding, to know how to do all manner of work for the service of the sanctuary, shall do according to all that the Lord has commanded.*"

This has brought me such peace. What He calls us to do, He does not expect us to do in our ability. He removes limitation and enables so that we can declare the reality of the resurrection of Jesus Christ; to begin to operate in the Spirit of wisdom.

WISDOM FOR SOLOMON'S TEMPLE

Before King David's death, he said to his son Solomon, "*Consider now, for the Lord has chosen you to build a house for the sanctuary; be strong and do it*" (1 Chron. 28:10), One of the Hebrew words for *strong* means "to be of good courage." Do you want to be of good courage and not be fearful? The world needs to see a courageous Church operating in God's strength.

Then David gave his son Solomon the plans for the vestibule, its houses, its treasuries, its upper chambers, its inner chambers, and the place of the mercy seat; and the plans for all that he had by the Spirit, of the courts of the house of the Lord, of all the chambers all around, of the treasuries of the house of God, and of the treasuries for the dedicated things....“All this,” said David, “the Lord made me understand in writing, by His hand upon me, all the works of these plans” (1 Chronicles 28:11-12;19).

David said, “Here Solomon, take the heavenly blueprints for this huge, beautiful, immaculate, detailed temple from the Holy Spirit. I want you to build this.” Who gave David the plans by which to build? The Holy Spirit did.

First Kings 6 gives the Lord’s instructions for building the temple. What amazes me is every little detail! Have you ever started reading about the temple? You just start skipping over some of it. I know I’m not the only one who has ever done that! It lists all the colors, cubits, and this and that. It was all very detailed. The temple was magnificent. People came from all over the world to behold its beauty, and they were amazed.

How would you like to be handed a set of plans from the Lord? I would venture to say that a lot of the things had not even been built at the time. Can you imagine Solomon thinking, *Hmm?*

Have you ever felt that way when you sense the call of God? Now, be honest. Maybe you received a prophetic word, and you think, *Hmm. This is a little bit too big for me.* The temple was bigger than Solomon’s ability, and much of the creative ability and craftsmanship wasn’t evident on the earth at the time. But Solomon had details from God, down to the very cubit and color. They were very important.

Just as God gave Moses the pattern for the first tabernacle, He also gave David and Solomon the pattern for the temple. When God gives you a vision, it is bigger than you. You know that you need the Spirit of wisdom to do it. We need it on an everyday basis—not just the gift, but taking it into a deeper union of the Kingdom flow:

> *If anyone speaks, let him speak as the oracles of God. If anyone ministers, let him do it as with the ability which God supplies, that in all things God may be glorified through Jesus Christ, to whom belong the glory and the dominion forever and ever* (1 Peter 4:11).

I want to finish and to build everything according to God's blueprints that were fashioned for me. The Bible says to leave an inheritance to your children's children. I want to leave my kids some money, but more than that, I would rather leave a spiritual inheritance of what I built according to God's blueprint for me.

Second Chronicles 1:6 says, "*And Solomon went up there to the bronze altar before the Lord, which was at the tabernacle of meeting, and offered a thousand burnt offerings on it.*" This is so incredible to me! Solomon had received detailed plans and I'm sure it was overwhelming. Then in this Scripture he is offering up a sacrifice to the Lord of 1,000 bulls, which is exceedingly above and beyond what was required. He did this because he said, "I need to see what I can do above and beyond."

Second Corinthians 9:10 says that as we give, not only will we reap a harvest in our seed, but we will receive a spiritual harvest as well. It's not that we are trying to buy something, but in sacrificial giving we are committing everything to it.

In Solomon's offering he was saying, "My father David said the Holy Spirit visited him and gave him these plans, and he told me to take them." This was the blueprint of Heaven. This wasn't natural wisdom. It required heavenly knowledge. Nothing in the natural could even begin to compare to what he had just been given.

That is what we need to realize in the Church. The enticement of this world's system should not be able to lure us if we put value on the greatest, most precious gift we have been given—His holy presence.

After Solomon made this great offering, he had a visitation from God, who asked what He could give the new king. Solomon could have asked God for riches, but read what he asked for:

> *You have shown great mercy to David my father, and have made me king in his place. Now, O Lord God, let Your promise to David my father be established, for You have made me king over a people like the dust of the earth in multitude. Now give me wisdom and knowledge"* (2 Chronicles 1:8-10a).

That word *established* is important. Romans 1:11a says, "*For I long to see you, that I may impart to you some spiritual gift, so that you may be established."* When Solomon had his visitation from God, he didn't ask for riches; he asked for wisdom so that God's plans could be established.

> *Then God said to Solomon: "Because this was in your heart, and you have not asked riches or wealth or honor or the life of your enemies, nor have you asked long life—but have asked wisdom and knowledge for yourself, that you may judge My people over whom I have made you king—wisdom and knowledge are granted to you"* (2 Chronicles 1:11-12a).

SPIRIT OF WISDOM IN THE NEW TESTAMENT

Jesus' Examples of Wisdom

When the Sabbath had come, He began to teach in the synagogue. And many hearing Him were aston-ished, saying, "Where did this Man get these things? And what wisdom is this which is given to Him, that such mighty works are performed by His hands!" (Mark 6:2)

They were blown away, not only by His wisdom, but also by the results of His teaching. Jesus received courses of action from the Father to live by every day. It was not just once in awhile. He was plugged in, so His life, on a day-to-day basis, demonstrated skillful living that glorified and the Kingdom of God.

Another place that shows how Jesus operated in the Spirit of wisdom is found in Luke 24. After Jesus was raised from the dead, He was walking toward the town of Emmaus with two disciples who didn't recognize Him. During their conversation, Jesus pre-tended to be unaware of His own crucifixion. *"And He said to them, 'What things?' So they said to Him, 'The things concern-ing Jesus of Nazareth, who was a Prophet mighty in deed and word before God and all the people'"* (Luke 24.19). Now the word *deed* there means "courses of action." They said, *"Jesus, who was mighty in courses of action and mighty in word before God and man."*

Also, Luke 2:52 says, *"And Jesus increased in wisdom and stature, and in favor with God and men."* He didn't just have it, but He increased in wisdom, and as a result it brought increase in favor with men, too. He received these mighty deeds from His Father's ideas. This is done through the Spirit of wisdom. If you start functioning out of the river of wisdom, then you too are going to find yourself having favor with God and men.

Paul's Spiritual Wisdom

Paul was the learned of the learned. He said, "I have learned above my contemporaries." But he depended on the Spirit to minister and to disciple his converts. His natural wisdom became nothing to him. He prayed this apostolic prayer for the Church: *"That the God of our Lord Jesus Christ, the Father of glory, may give to you the spirit of wisdom and of revelation in the knowledge of Him"* (Eph. 1:17). Not just the gift of wisdom, but the *Spirit* of wisdom. There is a big difference between the two.

Paul also prayed this:

> *For this reason we also, since the day we heard it, do not cease to pray for you, and to ask that you may be filled with the knowledge of His will in all wisdom and spiritual understanding; that you will walk worthy of the Lord, fully pleasing Him, being fruitful in every good work and increasing in the knowledge of God; strengthened with all might, according to His glorious power, for all patience and longsuffering with joy* (Colossians 1:9-11).

The word *filled* is the same terminology as "to be continually filled"—not a one-time filling. What does that look like, to be filled with the knowledge of His will?

Do you know that to fill something you have to pour into it? I have to pour liquid into a pitcher in order to pour it out. When you use wisdom, you will need more wisdom to fill you so you can continue to pour out. That is why we constantly have to be plugged in.

When you are operating in the Spirit of wisdom, you are walking in *creative ability*. You can't help but be fruitful, because it is not you anymore—it is Him through you. And it is God-given ability and comprehension of what He is showing you in the blueprints, and you can succeed because He is increasing through you.

If you begin to dissect it in the Greek, it says, "Be filled with a river of." When you are operating in the river of wisdom, you will be pleasing to God.

This process releases faith. You will want what God shows you; the unseen will be seen. In fact, it will cause dissatisfaction in anything else. I used to say, "Man, I am going to do my best to walk fully pleasing to God and to be fruitful in every good work." Paul says, "I just want you to be filled." Plugging into the Spirit of wisdom is impartation; this is the cure for striving.

WISDOM TESTIMONIES

Spirit of Wisdom and My Business

I remember how I got launched in the electrical business. I never went to school to learn to read schematics or any electronics. In fact, I didn't even graduate from high school. I quit and went into the army for two years. Then I began studying independently in our town's library. I got my journeyman's license, which usually takes four years. In only nine months I had my license and my own electrical business. I had never been an electrician; but I had God's favor on my life. I didn't know what favor was, but I was sure enjoying it!

My business really took off when a cattlefeed yard's batching computer quit working. The batching computer was what ran the feed mill to feed thousands of hungry cattle. When the mill isn't running, the management becomes very nervous. They usually had an expert come from out of town to repair the unit when it broke down, but the man could not get there because of a blizzard. Having been called out to repair it, I found I was in way over my head! At this point in my electrical career I was working on houses, running conduit, and small jobs. I was overwhelmed by the size of the feed mill's batching computer—it was so big that you could open the doors and step into it. It had 4" conduits with hundreds of wires coming out of it. So here I was, looking at this massive system with hundreds of working components. For the next three days I worked on it non-stop. I finally told them I had to go home and get some sleep. I went home perplexed; but that night in a dream, the Lord gave me the answer. In the dream I actually saw myself fixing the problem. I woke and quickly drove out to the feed mill. The Lord had showed me specifically to insert a spring on the back side, and I was easily able to fix it. All of sudden I was the hero of the day. The feed yard said I needed to fix all their stuff, but I didn't even know how I had repaired the batching computer! The Spirit of wisdom supernaturally showed me how to do it! My business grew from a one-person operation to several crews overnight!

The Lord blessed me with an ability to do things in the electrical field that caused CEOs of corporations to ask, "How are you doing this stuff? How do you know this?" And I believe it was the Spirit of wisdom in my life that was giving me the ability to do it. I would confound people because they would say, "You never went to school, you never got training, and nobody ever showed you how to do any of this?" I said, "No, nobody ever showed me how to do any of this. This is all supernatural ability."

The Lord gave me dreams with downloads on how to build equipment, and then my employees would stay busy for two years selling those products. One thing I invented was a well guard, and they are all over the country now. I made them from scratch when nobody even had any idea what a well guard was. The guards cost about $500 each to make, and I sold them for $3,000 plus labor. My employees and I could not even keep up with the orders. I never knew a slow time in business. I ended up having two shops in two towns. Major companies from all over the country called me to fix their equipment. It was a supernatural enabling by the Lord that I could do these things.

Because I was so blessed in business, I began to have influence in our community. God wants to give the Church influence in your community. And I believe that the Lord wants to do something, through the Church that brings double honor to Him. Would you like the Lord to release to you a river of wisdom that enables you to operate beyond your ability and empowers you to operate out of God's wisdom for your life? Would you like the Lord to pour out a river of wisdom for you? How about creative inventions?

The Lord wants to restore the Church to become leaders again in the areas of music and creative arts—to set the standards in the Church and in business. Some Christians have seen revelations through various types of prophetic encounters, and the Lord has given them creative ideas. It has taken them a season to develop them, but over the next several years they will come to fruition. Some of these will be in the area of energy for heat, fuel, electricity and many other creative inventions. In the medical field I believe we will see great breakthroughs by Christian doctors. In Deuteronomy 8:18, there is an anointing to make wealth, a supernatural ability from the Lord to see wealth for the establishing of the covenant. The Lord wants to release billions of dollars into Christian hands to finance the harvest throughout the nations. The Lord wants the Church to function in the Spirit of wisdom to see the release of things not seen. It is going to be fun to watch the Church become the forerunner in the business community instead of the tail end. Get ready to see a mighty river of the Spirit of wisdom in the area of music, art, movies, sounds, computers, and so much more!

The Lord wouldn't even allow me to begin to teach this information until I first experienced it. So it is more than just teaching; it's a conviction of my heart. I believe this is so tangible and real that every person can operate in a greater capacity. People will be astonished, and God will receive the glory. I am going to believe God to do that for you.

Lord, I thank You right now for releasing a mighty anointing of Deuteronomy 8:18 upon Your people for wealth for the harvest. Holy Spirit, we thank You for expressing through us the Spirit of wisdom in a mighty way. James 1:5 says that we can ask for wisdom and we will receive it. We ask with great confidence, knowing that if we ask anything according to Your will, You will hear us. If You hear us, then we know that You will grant our petitions. So with great joy we receive, right now, a mighty river of the Spirit of wisdom, so we may glorify Jesus in a mighty way! Amen.

CHAPTER 11

The Spirit of Understanding

U NDERSTANDING is the ability to put two and two together—what God shows you, you are then able to do. You are
able to move in wisdom and creative ability, because you understand and build according to the blueprints of Heaven.

> *He has filled him with the Spirit of God, in wisdom
> and understanding, in knowledge and all manner of
> workmanship, to design artistic works, to work in gold
> and silver and bronze, in cutting jewels for setting, in
> carving wood, and to work in all manner of artistic
> workmanship....He has filled them with skill to do all
> manner of work of the engraver and the designer and
> the tapestry maker, in blue, purple, and scarlet thread,
> and fine linen, and of the weaver—those who do every
> work and those who design artistic works* (Exodus
> 35:31-35).

What God asked Moses to do, nobody had ever before done
on earth. The Lord gave Moses the patterns and then released
the Spirit of wisdom into the craftsmen, so they would have
the creative ability to make the beautiful detailed items of the
tabernacle.

The Lord filled those who did the work with the Spirit of understanding, the spiritual perception to understand those plans. The Spirit of understanding and the Spirit of wisdom are paired together on the lampstand and flow together. God had given a command, but it took His wisdom and understanding to carry out this plan.

God put wisdom and understanding in every gifted artisan to accomplish all manner of work for the service of the sanctuary. The Spirit of understanding and the Spirit of wisdom operate in excellence so we can live life skillfully. What He asks us to do, He doesn't ask us to do in our ability. He takes off the lids of limitation and operates through our lives that confounds the world!

Daniel pressed into the things of the Lord. He had read the prophecies of Jeremiah, and he was seeking the Lord, fasting and praying. "*In those days I, Daniel, was mourning three full weeks. I ate no pleasant food, no meat or wine came into my mouth, nor did I anoint myself at all, till three whole weeks were fulfilled*" (Dan. 10:2-3). I believe there are many people right now in that same place—that place of setting their hearts toward God. "*So that you incline your ear to wisdom, and apply your heart to understanding*" (Prov. 2:2) They are saying, "God, I'm in a place where I want to know! I want to hear Your voice and meet with You. I want to hear from You and I want to know that I know that I know that what I'm hearing is Your voice."

Daniel was given the word of the Lord, but he didn't stop there. Many of us have words from God brewing in our lives. Many of us are in a new season; we are about to cross our Jordan, into another level of the promise and destiny God wants for our lives. We don't just need to know what that is, but we need the understanding and wisdom to walk it out.

Daniel set his heart towards this word, and as a result he had an angelic visitation. Daniel 10:6 talks about how the man's body was like beryl, his face like the appearance of lightning. Then,

> *Suddenly a hand touched me, which made me tremble on my knees and on the palms of my hand. And he said to me, "O Daniel, man greatly beloved, understand the words that I speak to you."…Then he said to me, "Do not fear, Daniel, for from the first day that you set your heart to understand, and to humble yourself before your God, your words were heard; and I have come because of your words….Now I have come to make you understand what will happen to your people in the latter days, for the vision refers to many days yet to come"* (Daniel 10:10-14).

The angel did not just come to give Daniel visitation, but understanding, the ability to comprehend and walk in understanding. Daniel didn't just want visitation, he wanted to understand, he wanted clarity in the call. And the Lord began to release the Spirit of understanding to Daniel.

I believe God is releasing a Spirit of understanding and wisdom to some of our past visitations and impartations; and also new impartation. I do not just want to know God's prophetic word; I want to walk it out! *"With Him are wisdom and strength, He has counsel and understanding"* (Job 12:13).

Isaiah 11:2 says, *"The Spirit of the Lord shall rest upon Him, the Spirit of wisdom and understanding, the Spirit of counsel and might, the Spirit of knowledge and of the fear of the Lord."* The kind of understanding God is talking about is a river of understanding—not just a small stream.

Do you want to build your life according to Heaven's blueprint? Do you want to be a wise master builder? *"Trust in the Lord with all your heart, and lean not on your own understanding;*

in all your ways acknowledge Him, and He shall direct your paths" (Prov. 3:5-6). Do you want the Lord to burn up the wood, hay, and stubble of your life so you can offer Him the pure silver and gold? From this day on, say, "I'm going to press in. I want wisdom and understanding for my life. I don't want to operate in a measure, but an increase from glory to glory."

This Spirit of wisdom and understanding will give you the ability to teach (see Exod. 35:34). Remember, it is not you, but Him. The best teaching flows out of the anointing—it will not dull the ears, because it will be powerful!

The Spirit of understanding gives clarity. Colossians 1:9 (AMP) says:

> *For this reason we also, from the day we heard of it, have not ceased to pray and make [special] request for you [asking] that you may be filled with the full (deep and clear) knowledge of His will in all spiritual wisdom [in comprehensive insight into the ways and purposes of God] and in understanding and discernment of spiritual things!*

> *In all wisdom and spiritual understanding; that you may walk worthy of the Lord, fully pleasing Him, being fruitful in every good work and increasing in the knowledge of God* (Colossians 1:9b-10).

Paul did not say, "Get more information." He said, "I'm going to pray for you to receive knowledge, wisdom and understanding."

It is not groping and hoping—it is God. It is authority and confidence. The disciples in Acts said they wanted to know God's predetermined will before the foundations of the earth so that they could speak with boldness. They didn't just want to speak the word; they wanted to know what they were talking about!

The word *boldness* is "confidence"! When we walk in the Spirit of understanding, we please the Lord.

When God imparts understanding, it comes to your inner man. Ephesians 1:18 says it causes the eyes of your understanding to be illuminated. You know what that means? Awakened, understanding, the hope of your call, and your inheritance. It causes a confidence and a holy boldness. Isaiah 32:15-17 says that when the Holy Spirit is poured out from on high, you dwell in that quiet assurance.

A few years ago, watching a speaker in a meeting, I thought he was one of the most arrogant persons I had ever heard. All of a sudden I heard the Lord say, "You call that pride? I call it confidence. What you've been calling humility has been a stench to My nostrils."

God wants us to operate in boldness and confidence! We are plugged right into the best connection; we are getting our information from the best possible source! We are receiving understanding from the One who can just speak a word and change the whole world. That should give us confidence. If God is for us, who can be against us?

This new season you are going into—you are not going in blind. God is going to give you the Spirit of understanding, with strategies and clarity. The Spirit of understanding breaks off fear!

Jesus operated in both the Spirit of understanding and the Spirit of wisdom. Even as a 12-year-old boy He had more understanding and wisdom than the learned Pharisees and Sadducees. When they heard Him, they marveled at His understanding, because it greatly exceeded theirs. He was blowing their minds.

It is time for us to become the light on the hill that raises up a standard. It's not by our ability but by being connected into the Spirit of understanding. *"Happy is the man who finds wisdom, and the man who gains understanding"* (Prov. 3:13).

I believe that the Lord is about to release power on the Church to operate in a fresh anointing of the Spirit of wisdom and understanding and to walk in His *dunamis* power. (*Dunamis* is a Greek word that means "might." I will discuss it more in the chapter on the Spirit of might.) God is going to enlighten you, to illuminate you. Job said that he walked as the Lord led his path, even in darkness (see Job 29:3). The world is becoming darker, and God's people are called to be the light.

I believe the Church is going to walk in double honor—that even the government will seek the Church's counsel regularly, as they did with Daniel. They knew he had the Spirit of excellence.

We know very little about God's intricate workings in creation, but by faith we understand that the universe was framed by the words of God. God did not make the universe out of nothing. He made it out of invisible things. Although His ways are invisible to us, they are not meaningless. By faith we know it is all clear in His eyes. This spiritual understanding causes us to know that we are safe when we follow Him. He knows what is coming even though we do not. Wisdom and understanding bring life to the soul (see Prov. 3:21-22).

We cannot relate to the ways of the Lord or the ways of others without understanding. It is understanding that causes compassion to flow from us. The Spirit of understanding allows us to look into something beyond the facts, and to know why it actually is the way it is. Luke 24:45 says that Jesus "*opened their* [the disciples'] *understanding, that they might comprehend the scriptures.*" Jesus brings to light—unveils, takes the cover off, discloses—the hidden things or the secret things of God.

The hidden treasures become known to you. You will receive insight into how God works. Understanding means a "putting together" or a comprehending or grasping of His Word. In other words, He "turns on the lights for us." How many times have you sat down to read God's Word and an hour later not remember a thing you read? In cases like these, the Spirit of understanding was not operating.

Psalm 119:27 is a good prayer: "*Make me understand the way of Your precepts; so shall I meditate on Your wonderful works.*" We must have God's understanding of His wisdom before we can begin to apply it to our lives and before we can pass it on to others.

Many Christians are stumbling today, partly, I believe, because they are ignorant—not only about what the Word of God says and what it requires, but also about our human motives, our wrong dependencies, our misconceived priorities, etc. As we read God's Word, it is the Spirit of understanding that will expose these things so we can deal with them. "...*People who do not understand will be trampled*" (Hos. 4:14).

The Spirit of understanding helps us to grasp the things of God's Kingdom. By faith we know them, but by the Spirit of understanding we learn to cherish them. The Spirit of understanding empowers us to dig deep into mysteries of the Kingdom. As we receive, we see a thirty, sixty, or one hundredfold of God's mysteries. Matthew 13:23 says, "*But he who received seed on the good ground is he who hears the word and understands it, who indeed bears fruit and produces; some a hundredfold, some sixty, some thirty.*" We are enabled by the Spirit of understanding to comprehend the Word that has been released.

Here are some Scriptures regarding the Spirit of understanding:

> *But the Helper, the Holy Spirit, whom the Father will send in My name, He will teach you all things, and bring to your remembrance all things that I said to you* (John 14:26).

And we know that the Son of God has come and has given us an understanding, that we may know Him who is true; and we are in Him who is true, in His Son Jesus Christ. This is the true God and eternal life (1 John 5:20).

The eyes of your understanding being enlightened; that you may know what is the hope of His calling, what are the riches of the glory of His inheritance in the saints (Ephesians 1:18).

That their hearts may be encouraged, being knit together in love, and attaining to all riches of the full assurance of understanding, to the knowledge of the mystery of God, both of the Father and of Christ (Colossians 2:2).

Consider what I say, and may the Lord give you understanding in all things (2 Timothy 2:7).

Holy Spirit, I invite You to come and pour out Your Spirit of understanding, to fill us with a river of it! Release a connection with Your heart and Your thoughts, so we can understand exactly what You say. Spirit of understanding, give us clarity in Jesus' name. Spring forth, rivers of wisdom and understanding! I pray for activation. Flow like rivers of living water. Holy Spirit, take the limits off so we can say, "Anything is possible with You!"

CHAPTER 12

The Spirit of Counsel

I love the counsel of the Lord and I seek it daily! I want to know the intent of His mind, thoughts, and heart, because I want to build my life and fulfill my destiny according to the counsel of Heaven. I won't move an inch without the friendly counsel of God over my tent—my family, ministry, and life. Why? Because the Spirit of counsel unlocks my destiny!

> "Eye has not seen, nor ear heard, nor have entered into the heart of man the things which God has prepared for those who love Him." But God has revealed them to us through His Spirit. For the Spirit searches all things, yes, the deep things of God (1 Corinthians 2:9-10).

The Spirit of counsel casts off restraints and gives me certainty and assurance in my steps. I rely not on myself, but on Him. "'For My thoughts are not your thoughts, nor are your ways My ways,' says the Lord. 'For as the heavens are higher than the earth, so are My ways higher than your ways, and My thoughts than your thoughts'" (Isa. 55:8-9).

Proverbs 11:14 says that where there is no counsel, people fall. I don't want to fall! I want to be sure of my steps. By the Holy Spirit, the Spirit of counsel, I am able to see God's ways and know

His thoughts toward me. I am glad that His thoughts and His ways are higher than mine!

RIVERS OF COUNSEL

God wants us to desire His deep, friendly counsel—to be dissatisfied with the shallow and hunger for the deep. Job once moved in such an anointing that the rock poured rivers of oil for him and his path was like butter:

> *Oh, that I were as in months past, as in the days when God watched over me; when His lamp shone upon my head, and when by His light I walked through darkness; just as I was in the days of my prime, when the friendly counsel of God was over my tent; when the Almighty was yet with me, when my children were around me; when my steps were bathed with cream [butter], and the rock poured out rivers of oil for me!"* (Job 29:2-6)

God's intimate friendship rested on his tent. As Job remembered God's glory, he recognized that God was the source of his prosperity and happiness. God illuminated his steps through life's darkness. *"Your word is a lamp to my feet and a light to my path"* (Ps. 119:105).

Would you like to live in such an anointing where the lamp of God's favor shines upon you? Ask God for a Job 29 impartation in your life. Ask Him for the rock to pour out a river of counsel in your life. A river is no small measure! Imagine rivers of oil—not just a little vial, but rivers.

The word *counsel* means "secret." *Tent* means "tabernacle." God lives in you, so the tent is you. The Lord loves to reveal His secrets, His "deep things," to those who are His friends. "*The secret of the Lord is with those who fear Him, and He will show them His covenant.*" (Ps. 25:14).

As believers, we are His friends. Jesus said, "*No longer do I call you servants, for a servant does not know what his master is doing; but I have called you friends, for all things that I heard from My Father I have made known to you*" (John 15:15). He also said, "The Holy Spirit will show you of things to come." That John 15:15 realm is available right now! The deep things of God will catapult you into an entirely new dimension of intimacy with Him.

About six months after I was saved I discovered these passages about oil in the Book of Job. I showed my senior pastor and said, "Look here, I would like this rock to pour out rivers of oil on me. Let's ask for rivers of oil! How about it?" The thought of rivers of oil excited me. Once I started praying this way, God saturated me with His fresh oil.

I love the revelation my friend and colleague, Bobby Conner, had about the cream or butter. He said that the cream represents the Word, and the Word sets the path. The river of oil helps you slide down the path.

During a meeting in Meadville, Pennsylvania, two men, both devil worshipers and gang members, became born again. They were tough guys, but God messed up their plans. The deciding factor was His power, and man, did it hit them—*bam!* Down they went under His power, and then He saturated them in baby oil!

"What's this?" they cried in disbelief. It was oil! It was the Holy Spirit, and the baby oil symbolized they were but babes in the Lord. They both jumped to their feet, tore off their pentagrams, flung them to the ground, and said, "We want Jesus!"

Whether we are brand-new in the Lord or mature believers, God can bathe our paths with oil so that we slip and slide from the sheer volume of it. Let Him saturate you with rivers and rivers of oil so that it oozes off you wherever you go. One day, you'll make a squish-squash sound as you walk in the Lord, because you'll be so fat with the anointing. Are you ready to plump up?

SPEAKING HIS COUNSEL INTO OTHERS

God wants to bless you with the privilege of speaking His counsel into individuals around you, too. People are constantly trying to find answers about their lives—through misguided means such as psychics, witches, horoscopes, and Ouija boards. The Church has been given the opportunity to flow in a river of godly counsel that will answer people's questions and unlock their destinies. I believe the Church, in this hour, is called to raise up future generations to operate by the counsel of God. It is time for us to embrace the river of counsel that God wants to release on our lives!

What an evangelism tool. Imagine walking in such a deep flow of the Spirit of counsel that you receive words of knowledge for others. I see this happening in my own life more and more. I'll meet someone new, but with one look God reveals things about them to me that I have no other way of knowing. I recall a particular time in Houston. I was in my hotel room preparing for a large meeting. The Holy Spirit said, "Wait! I want to tell you something!" He gave me the name of a woman and the exact details of her medical problem. The Lord told me that this information would break open the meeting so that He could move powerfully. At the pulpit, I called out, "Is there a Maria here?"

When she came forward, I said, "The Lord gave me your name, and He said, 'You're waking up and this area of your body isn't

sore, but it's stiff and you're afraid you're going to be paralyzed.'"
Tears welled in her eyes.

"Maria, since God revealed it to me, He is more than able to
heal you!"

She lifted her leg up and down and she said, "Oh! I couldn't
raise my leg like this!"

Instant healing! The entire place broke wide open and God
instantly healed people. When I asked for those who knew the
Lord had healed them to raise their hands, arms waved all over
the room. I couldn't count them all. That is the counsel of God!

Many people live in a realm where they see things happen in
prayer before they actually happen in life. They are able to give
the exact word that could unlock Heaven for someone. There are
times when God gives someone else a word that can open up the
future for you. God wants us to live in that realm of counsel,
knowing the Father's mind and heart daily for our children, our
families, and our ministries. This river of counsel reveals the
secrets of the heart, causes people to come in, fall to their knees,
and say, "Surely, God is in this place." We are called to raise up
future generations by His counsel.

God can use you to unlock others' futures so they can see His
intent for their lives. God's counsel knows what He has planned
and purposed for every individual. God knows that our own
counsel and plans fall short. *"The Lord brings the counsel of the
nations to nothing; He makes the plans of the peoples of no
effect"* (Ps. 33:10).

It thrills me to know that God's ways are higher than mine
(see Isa. 55:8-9). I want to minister in meetings where the Holy
Spirit shows me beforehand what He wants to do. God's counsel
is so awesome that I see people already at the meeting hours
before they arrive. I love it! I want to reach such depths that His
manifest presence alone heals every sick person in a meeting. I

believe we can see that! Ask God to release the Spirit of counsel so that you will walk in greater things. Share God's counsel with the lost so that God can release their destiny, too.

My wife and I recently bought coffee at the drive-up window of the local Starbucks. The Lord instantly revealed to me several things about the daughter of the young man taking our order. As I began to share what the Lord told me, his mouth fell open in complete astonishment. We drove off, leaving him in a whirlwind of the Lord's thoughts toward him. A few days later we went to the same coffee shop. This same young man was outside at one of the tables drinking coffee. As soon as he saw me he said, "Who are you?" I was able to sit down with him and share about the Lord. The counsel of the Lord will make a way, when there is no way!

William Branham walked the slippery path and obtained the key. He knew that he could plug into the intent of the Father's mind and heart for a specific meeting, and then, power would be release seeing incredible healing, and miracles taking place. When God reveals His counsel, He also releases the anointing of power and might to see His counsel fulfilled!

ANTICIPATE HIS COUNSEL

The counsel of God is also the ability to comprehend whatever God reveals—whether for you personally or for those around you.

A time is coming in the Church of Christ where the prophetic will flow in such a way that the intents of the heart will be revealed. God wants you to flow in the Spirit of counsel in such a way that you will know His mind and heart for your life.

Psalm 139:17-18 says that the sums of His thoughts are like sand on the seashore, and they are precious to me. When I wake up in the morning His thoughts are there with me. Do you want to live in that realm? Do you want a river of counsel, to know the thoughts of God toward you? Are you ready to get out of the shallow and into the deep things of God?

By the Holy Spirit, we can know His ways, and know His thoughts toward us. It's not enough to hear, read about, or think about the Holy Spirit. We have to *know* Him, because He desires us to understand, enjoy, and minister out of that fullness.

The Bible says that God has fashioned your days and written your life's books (see Ps. 139:16). You are His workmanship, and He has ordained you for good works (see Eph. 2:10; John 14:12). We may plan our way, but God is the one who directs our steps, and His plan is for us to build our lives according to the blueprint of Heaven! "*The counsel of the Lord stands forever, the plans of His heart to all generations*" (Ps. 33:11).

The Spirit of counsel is God's direction and instruction concerning life and daily living. He points the way and instructs us how to get there. We can have confidence that He will not withhold His counsel from us. King David revealed that God guided him with His counsel (see Ps. 73:24).

Another key is that David waited for God's counsel. "*I wait for the Lord, my soul waits, and in His word, I do hope. My soul waits for the Lord more than those who watch for the morning, yes, more than those who watch for the morning*" (Ps. 130:5-6). I love that Scripture. David is saying, "I eagerly and earnestly wait for a word from God." He waits with such anticipation for God's word like those who say, "I can't wait until tomorrow! I can't wait for God to reveal the next river of His counsel!"

Every day I wake up and think, *Today I am going to learn something new from Jesus. I am so hungry, Jesus. The Bible says*

I am not supposed to live on yesterday's manna. I am supposed to live on every word that precedes from Your mouth (see Deut. 8:3). *I am hungry for Your Word today—a river of Your counsel.*

To be honest, studying God's Word can often be a challenge. But when God imparts that *rhema* word to you, it becomes an encounter. *Rhema* is Greek for the word that means "to do" or "to become." Through the *rhema* word, we can know our future. It's the word of power and anointing. We live and thrive by the *rhema* word. "*You also gave Your good Spirit to instruct them, and did not withhold Your manna from their mouth, and gave them water for their thirst*" (Neh. 9:20). The word *instruct* in this context means "to have success, to prosper, and to guide wittily." The Holy Spirit guides and leads you and shows you the way. He releases divine counsel (His *rhema* word) and it flows like a river to you, for you, and through you.

I have had encounters with God through the Word that were just as powerful as any other encounter. In the counsel of God is a treasure chest of richness, wisdom, and understanding. I don't just desire the nuggets of this treasure; I want the gold! Early on in my Christian walk, during those months of intense training with the Lord, the Holy Spirit made Himself so real I began to *know* Him.

This is for everyone. God wants to break open the rivers of His counsel in the life of every believer. He wants us to *walk* in the unlimited anointing of the Holy Spirit—all of the time. It wasn't just for the saints of old. It's not just for evangelists. This river of oil is for you, your life, your family, and your destiny.

WALKING IN HIS COUNSEL

God has predetermined His plans, purposes, and destiny for us: "*To do whatever Your hand and Your purpose determined before to be done*" (Acts 4:28). He performs His secret will, the counsel of His will, the hidden purpose of His heart. His hand and His purpose determined our destiny. This brings us true peace, knowing that whatever comes our way has passed through God's hand first.

However, we must wait for His counsel, or we will experience leanness in our souls. "*They* [the Hebrew people] *soon forgot His works; they did not wait for His counsel, but lusted exceedingly in the wilderness, and tested God in the desert. And He gave them their request, but sent leanness into their soul*" (Ps. 106:13-15). The Israelites were impatient and forgot their dependence on God to fulfill their destiny and purpose. They didn't wait for His wisdom, counsel, and providence. Even though God granted their request, their souls became lean.

Many of God's people live in a spirit of leanness because they haven't learned how to wait for the counsel of God. They haven't understood nor grabbed hold of it.

God's plans and purposes are unchangeable, and the Bible tells us we are wise to listen to His counsel and receive instruction (Prov. 19:20). Only God's Word stands the test of time and eternity and sustains us. All of God's purposes will be accomplished in His timing.

THE DISCIPLES PUSH IN FOR COUNSEL

The disciples were equipped and trained, and they received impartation from the very best—Jesus. Every day they ministered with and learned from the One who had the unlimited anointing of the Holy Spirit. They listened with awe as He shared the depths of the living Word, and they saw great and mighty things. Jesus told them, "*Most assuredly, I say to you, he who believes in Me, the works that I do he will do also; and greater works than these he will do, because I go to My Father"* (John 14:12).

Acts 2-3 relates a powerful outpouring of the Holy Spirit, of which the disciples were witnesses. In Acts 4:28, we see them in one accord, before the Lord, crying to receive His divine counsel, *"To do whatever Your hand and Your purpose determined before to be done."* Purpose in this context signifies "advice, will and counsel." They asked the Lord to reveal His purpose in the plan of God for the salvation of man through Christ. They wanted to know the content of His divine plan.

They knew, through walking with Jesus for three and one-half years, that they could receive this divine counsel from the Father who knows all things. They knew that if He revealed His plans, He would carry them out—that the river of counsel would flow as living waters.

When God released the counsel of Heaven, a mighty river of anointing poured out upon them afresh. *"And when they had prayed, the place where they were assembled together was shaken; and they were all filled with the Holy Spirit, and they spoke the word of God with boldness"* (Acts 4:31).

In John 21:1-14, we see a powerful example of divine counsel in the lives of the disciples. Having fished all night and caught nothing, they reluctantly obeyed Jesus' command to cast the net on the other side of the boat. You know the rest of the story. The net was so full they could not raise it! That, my friends, is going from *nothing* to overflow. The overflow happened because they followed the advice of the Wonderful Counselor, who in turn imparted a plentiful harvest. Please notice that that it was John who recognized the Lord (see John 21:7). John was known as the one who laid his head on the Master's chest. He wanted to know Jesus' heart and mind. That is counsel.

WE CAN RECEIVE COUNSEL

We can live in this same flow of the river of counsel moment by moment, hour by hour, day by day. We can build our destiny according to the wise Master Builder's plans. The Spirit of counsel, the Holy Spirit, reveals those things Jesus declares for us. (See John 16:13.)

In Acts 20:27, Paul, speaking to the elders of the church, said, *"For I have not shunned to declare to you the whole counsel of God."* In other words, Paul is saying, "I received these plans from the Spirit of counsel who has taken what the Wonderful Counselor, Jesus (see Isa. 9:6), has declared, for He reveals the Father's plans!"

CHAPTER 13

The Spirit of Might

THE Spirit of counsel and the Spirit of might are paired together. The counsel of God releases the Spirit of might.

The might of God is the *vigor and strength of God*—not only *in* you, but also *upon* you to fulfill the heavenly blueprint He has for your life. Your inner man is strengthened to such an extent that you know, without a doubt, that you "*can do all things through Christ who strengthens* [you]" (Phil. 4:13). You can wake up in the morning with fresh strength to walk through life as an *overcomer*, not as one who is overcome. We can live deeply rooted in the flow of His Spirit of might, and it does not matter what storm blows. God never meant for us to be tossed to and fro, but He intends us to walk in His Spirit of might!

The *counsel* of God is what releases the *might* of God. Remember, counsel and might are paired together in Isaiah 11:2. These are not just gifts of the Spirit, but they are actually ceaseless rivers that flow from Heaven through your life, part of the sevenfold Spirit of God.

Jesus' names are *Wonderful Counselor*, and *Mighty God* (see Isaiah 9:6). These names clearly display the relationship of counsel with releasing the mighty acts of God.

I believe Caleb and Joshua operated in the realm of the Spirit of might; they had the counsel of God as well. God had aid to them, "I give you Canaan. It is yours, and I give you everything in it." That is why they were able to say to the other leaders about the land, "*We are well able to overcome it*" (Num. 13:30b). God then gave them His might so they were able to go in and possess what He had shown them. He *revealed* His plans through His counsel, and they were able to *carry them out* because He equipped them with His *might*.

The others could not grasp or operate in God's might. They were afraid of the giants.

PAUL'S PRAYERS FOR POWER

That He would grant you, according to the riches of His glory, to be strengthened with might through His Spirit in the inner man, that Christ may dwell in your hearts through faith; that you, being rooted and grounded in love, may be able to comprehend with all the saints what is the width and length and depth and height—to know the love of Christ which passes knowledge; that you may be filled with all the fullness of God. Now to Him who is able to do exceedingly abundantly above all that we ask or think, according to the power that works in us (Ephesians 3:16-20).

We can learn several things from this incredible passage! Paul prayed, "*That He would grant you, according to the riches of His glory, to be strengthened with might through His Spirit in the inner man, that Christ may dwell in your hearts through faith.*" It's awesome to know that you can walk in Christ's stature and strength.

"*...that you, being rooted and grounded in love, may be able to comprehend with all the saints what is the width and* *length and depth and height—to know the love of Christ which passes knowledge, that you may be filled with all the fullness of God."* Wow! Do you want to be filled with *all* the fullness of God? The word *fullness* literally means "to be crammed full; weighted down."You can live on a day-to-day basis in a new realm of His glory and the weightiness of His presence so that you begin to diffuse His fragrance.

"Now to Him who is able to do exceedingly abundantly above all that we ask or think, according to the power that works in us." The Lord wants to do big, big things, don't you think?

Now, go back to Ephesians 3:16, because I want to show you something else. Paul prayed for the Lord's *strength*. He first of all said, *"that He would grant you."* The word *grant* there means "to bestow a gift, or supply or furnish something that is necessary." Paul says "I pray that the Father would give you something according to the riches of His glory"

Don't you know God is pretty rich? Do you want to be wealthy in the things of the Kingdom? Riches and wealth represent abundance! So Paul is saying, "Listen, I'm praying that Father God would give to you out of the abundance of His glory."What is glory? The glory is who He is. It is the weightiness of who He is. He's saying, "I'm asking the Father to give you an abundance of His weighty glory! The word *abundance* means "continuous supply." Do you want to operate out of the strength of the Lord on a continuous, day-to-day basis?

KRATOS POWER

"To be strengthened with might through His Spirit in the inner man" (Eph. 3:16). The word strengthen comes from the

Greek word *kratos*, which means "power; Kingdom manifestation of dominion."

Kratos is the power, might, or ability to strengthen you in your *inner man*. It gives you strength over temptation. It's the manifestation of Kingdom dominion in you. What does that mean? It means that the things which are taking place in the natural don't rule your life because Jesus is ruling and reigning by the *kratos* of the Lord! We've got to walk steadfastly in the things of the Lord.

Paul says, "I want you to walk in a realm where you have strength to overcome persecution, cares and concerns, and strength to minister in the anointing. Strength to walk out what He has for your life, strength to walk in your destiny, and strength to stand and say, 'Now, behold, the Lord your God!' I want Him to do things in your life that are exceedingly abundantly above and beyond what you can even think or imagine, according to His mighty power, and that you begin to bring God glory." When Christ rules and reigns in your inner self, you will stand strong in the things of the Lord.

Paul uses *kratos* again in Ephesians 6:10, "*Finally, my brethren, be strong in the Lord and in the* **power** [kratos] *of His might.*" He's saying, "Right *now* be strong in His *kratos* power." The Lord is releasing powerful dimensions of His anointing upon the Body of Christ right now! We're about to see and do incredible things in cities that will transform regions—by *kratos* allowing Christ to rule and reign in you. Even though the outward is perishing, you're getting stronger within (see 2 Cor. 4:16).

Let's look at a few examples of *kratos* in Jesus' life. When Jesus ministered in the anointing, He got the religious people stirred up. They took stones to kill Him! And Jesus just walked right past them unharmed. Do you know what the other 12 were doing? They didn't run away. The 12 of them were walking right behind Him like ducklings. The religious people couldn't touch

Jesus. He didn't get upset because He knew His purpose, and He had Kingdom dominion in His inner man.

John 18:5-6 tells how the soldiers came to arrest Jesus in the Garden of Gethsemane. As soon as He identified Himself as the one they sought, His Kingdom manifested, and they all fell to the ground! This is a picture of His *kratos* dominion.

Kratos can act like a nuclear explosion of God's Kingdom and dominion in a city or region. Acts 19:8 describes Paul's giving the Ephesians the counsel of God. He preached the Kingdom, both renewing their minds and persuading their hearts. It says that two years after he began preaching in Ephesus, *"the word of God grew mightily and prevailed"* (Acts 19:20). The word for "mightily" there is *kratos*. A Kingdom explosion took place in Ephesus. It was such a great manifestation of the Kingdom that everything not of the Kingdom had to fall. Paul preached under the flow of the counsel and might of the Lord. We want that same kind of power to come to and through our lives and ministries! Do it, Lord!

DUNAMIS POWER

Kratos is also found in Ephesians 1:19. *Kratos* is actually only one of four Greek words that mean "might" or "power." *Dunamis* is another Greek word that means "might," and it is also found in this passage. It is the first word "power" mentioned in this sentence. Here is how it reads: *"And what is the exceeding greatness of His **power** [dunamis] toward us who believe, according to the working of His mighty **power** [kratos]."* While *kratos* means God's power ruling *within* us, *dunamis* refers to God's power *upon* the believer's life. *Dunamis* is the power that enabled Jesus and His disciples to do miracles, signs and wonders. It refers to mighty acts of power. It empowers believers today to do the same as well. The Spirit of counsel releases the Spirit of might, and a river of the miraculous will begin to explode for the glory of Jesus!

Colossians 1:11a says, "*Strengthened with all might, according to His glorious power.*" The word for "strengthened with all might" is *dunamis*. In the phrase "*according to His glorious power,*" the word for power is *kratos*, God's Kingdom dominion within. So the power He gives us within by His might enables us to walk in the anointing for mighty deeds. We need God's strength and might to rule in us inwardly in order to handle the anointing of power.

In Ephesians 3:16, both Greek words are used. It reads, "*That He would grant you, according to the riches of His glory, to be strengthened* [kratos] *with might* [dunamis] *through His Spirit in the inner man.*" Again, God will strengthen us within with *kratos* (inward power) in order for us to carry His *dunamis* power (outward power), for mighty deeds.

FINISHERS ARISE!

God wants to increase your might! Be faithful with what has been given to you, and you will get more. Ask the Lord to release His might for you. Second Timothy 2:1 says, "*Therefore, my son, be strong in the grace that is in Christ Jesus.*" That is how we are strong—through His grace. Begin to recognize God's grace. Ephesians 3:7 says we are effective ministers because we minister according to the grace that has been given to us.

This is God's intention for you. You can live victoriously—not beaten down, hoping to just make it through. You can do all things through Christ who strengthens you! Be strong in the might and the power of the Lord!

The Spirit of might takes you from the beginning of salvation all the way through the process of maturing, putting off the old man, walking in the new man, and walking in the fullness of Him. How do you finish strong in the Lord? You do this by living in the anointing of His might. Psalm 92:12-14 says that even in your old age you will be like a green olive tree bearing much fruit if you dwell in the house of God. If you are a born-again Christian, God is your Father, and Christ leads you in His triumph by the power of His Spirit's might (see 2 Cor. 2:14). You are called to declare a victory cry with the army of the Lord! And when the enemy hears this sound, he will retreat! We are not going to be overcome. We are overcomers!

THE ANGEL OF MIGHT

Prophetic encounters are definitely valid, and the Bible is full of visions, dreams, and trances. We don't try to make these experiences happen, but God allows them to happen as we worship and press in to know Him

Angel in Houston

In one of our conferences in Houston, Texas, I was to speak one morning. During the early morning hours in my hotel room, I felt the presence of the same massive angel I had seen in my office. He didn't say a thing; I just knew he was there. That day as I preached, there was an awesome anointing of might. Right in the middle of my preaching, I decreed, "The Lion of Judah rules and reigns, and we're proclaiming the roar of the Lord!"

Everyone there jumped up and began declaring the roar of the Lord. It was so intense! After several minutes, I tried to get the people to sit down, but the Lord said "You're done preaching."

I said, "Never mind; I'm done."

Once I was sharing about the counsel of God that releases the might of God. Incredibly, the entire audience came running up to the front. I mean, they literally ran! Then all of a sudden, the big angel was standing on the platform! The anointing was so intense that I had to stop. The swirling of the power of the Holy Spirit was so strong upon me that as I walked through the people, they were being thrown down by the power of the might of God. Not one or two, but 10 to 15 at a time. I had to get back on the platform, because I was afraid that people would get hurt. Several people were instantly healed and hundreds of lives changed.

Might Increases Faith

After the same service in which the massive angel was present, several pastors who had been present told me that they felt a major shift had taken place, and at that moment they felt they could ask the Lord for *anything* and it would happen. One of the manifestations of the Spirit of might is boldness that releases *great faith* to believe for the impossible to become possible at that moment! When you begin to live in this realm, your faith increases on a daily basis. You become stronger. With this confidence and strength comes a Holy Ghost boldness that you will not be denied!

In another meeting, as I began to share, I instantly felt the Spirit of might begin to flow. One of the other keynote speakers literally jumped onto the platform and said, "There is such a powerful atmosphere of faith in this place." This was true, but it was more than just the gift of faith, it was the explosion of the Spirit of might that was released in the room. It was the very *vigor* or strength of the Lord flowing like a mighty river. In those moments, I felt like I was 50 feet tall and anything could happen!

It was the explosion of the King's domain that released the strength to believe for *anything*.

This is exactly what happened when David confronted the giant Goliath. He wasn't afraid or intimidated by the size or the words of Goliath. Because he was operating out of the Spirit of might, he saw Goliath as the grasshopper, instead of himself. I can see David as a young man, up against the larger, experienced, battle-tested Goliath. David had great strength, boldness, and confidence. "Is this who you are afraid of? Does he not know who he speaks against? Watch now as you behold the might of God!" Down came the giant. Fear gripped the hearts of the Philistines as they watched their mighty champion fall before a young boy with a sling and a stone. (Read the entire account in First Samuel 17.)

The might of God is the very strength of God Himself. Isaiah 52:10 says, "*The Lord has made bare His holy arm in the eyes of all the nations; and all the ends of the earth shall see the salvation of our God.*" We've seen the finger of God, we've seen the hand of God, but we're about to see the *arm* of God! His arm represents His *power*. How strong is God? If you had to measure the strength of God, could you? Can He lift the weight of the world? Can He carry the sin of the world? Yes, He has already proven He can do that and more. God has unlimited strength, and when we get a revelation of this, our faith goes up. We know that anything is possible because He is so mighty! He wants His might to flow through us daily, not just every once in a while, but every day! Let the river of might flow!

MIGHT IS FOR ALL

The Lord intends for every believer to minister out of a strong anointing. Paul said, "*And my speech and my preaching were not with persuasive words of human wisdom, but in demon-stration of the Spirit and of power*" (1 Cor. 2:4). That is how we should live. The Lord wants to take the good news out of the church building and into the world around us. The key is that He will not do it by our power, but by the power of the Holy Spirit. It is His desire to invade the marketplace, the schools, the prisons, etc. He will give us the ability to see those things and the might to carry them out. Our response should simply be, "OK, let it be done unto me according to what You have said (Your counsel)."

He wants to increase His anointing—not somebody else's anointing, not your own ability, but His anointing on your life. He wants you to operate in such a realm of His might that it causes others to say, "That has to be God with them." Ask God for that kind of anointing on your life, on your ministry, on your business, and your family!

Are you ready to see great power? Are you *desperate* to see great power? That desire is burning in me! In our ministry, we're seeing incredible things right now. It's an accelerated time. I'm amazed at my own meetings! God wants to do something through your life that causes others to marvel. We need to say, "Lord, according to Your Word, we ask for the exceeding great-ness of Your power through our lives, so we begin to see the 'above-and-beyond'" (see Eph. 3:20). God wants to do for us just like He told Moses He would do regarding Israel—He promised to do something so great in their lives that the nations would marvel. We need power and might, and we need to decree the reality of the Kingdom on a daily basis.

It's time to believe for the impossible to be possible. If you are involved in any kind of ministry and have had meetings with a hundred people, how about asking the Lord for a thousand? Let's begin to believe for our cities. If you have had a meeting with a 100,000 people, why not believe for a whole nation? How much can you believe for? But—when God answers your prayers and gives you a river of anointing of His might, what are you going to do with what you get?

God wants to bring increase in your life. He wants a hundred-fold increase. He wants your life to make an impact on the world around you. He wants these things for the here and now. He wants you to marvel at how He uses your life. Every time that I've gone to another level in God, it has released an attitude of graciousness, gratitude, and humility that I could never produce myself. My lips can't help but speak of His lovingkindness. I pray God opens up a river of might to you right now for your daily life for impact in the Kingdom!

In summary, God's might is the activation process that gives us the power to carry out His will. (See Isaiah 46:10-11 and Psalm 18:32.) We have been made *"more than conquerors through Him who loved us"* (Rom. 8:37), and the victory by which we overcome is our faith (see 1 John 5:4). It is through faith that we choose to allow the performance of His will in our lives, and it is by faith that we get the confidence that He will perform it. So His might produces faith within us.

The Spirit of might *within* us (*kratos*) is the power that enables us to put off the habits of our flesh and crucify it with its passions, and to put on Christ (see 1 Cor. 7:37 and Gal. 5:13,16). The Spirit of might *upon* us [*dunamis*] brings the mighty acts of power: strength, miracles, signs, and wonders. Ask the Lord to awaken the eyes of your heart to the mighty power that is working in and through you.

The meaning of *might* could be put like this: the anointing, or God's valor, strength, and power through your life to be able to fulfill that which He has purposed. Remember, Zechariah 4:6 says, "Not by our might, not by our strength, not by our power, but by the Holy Spirit." Wouldn't you like the Lord to open up to you today a new level of might? He's ready!

All your works shall praise You, O Lord, And Your saints shall bless You. They shall speak of the Glory of Your Kingdom, And talk of Your Power, To make known to the sons of men His Mighty acts, and the glorious majesty of His kingdom. Your kingdom is an everlasting kingdom, and Your dominion endures throughout all generations. (Psalm 145:10-13).

When you function out of the Spirit of might you will see the dominion of the Kingdom being released through your life in such a way that you manifest the power of the Kingdom. The Lord wants you to plug into His might to see the mighty acts of God through your life. He wants a river of might to flow out of you that will release the mighty acts of God so that people will see the manifestation of the Kingdom in power and they will see and behold the glory and power of the Kingdom. That is what the Spirit of Might is. A river of the manifest dominion of the King and His Kingdom through your life. It is impact. As it is in Heaven so shall it be upon the earth.

CHAPTER 14

The Spirit of Knowledge

ONE morning I had to get up at 5 o'clock and go to work. I noticed that my truck needed oil. Just as I began to add the oil, I felt the tangible presence of the Lord. Awe washed over me, as I realized what was happening. A voice gently pierced through the morning quietness and said, "Turn around." I knew it was God; my skin tingled and every hair stood on end as I swung around to greet Him. But my eyes met light—thousands upon thousands of twinkling stars draped across the velvet black sky. I craned my head back to take it all in—what a great expanse of stars! It was beautiful and awesome, in the greatest sense. Then a star freed itself from the rest, and shot across the sky from east to west. I followed it with my eyes until I couldn't see it anymore. Wonder and then awe surged from deep within as I became aware of the vastness of God through my spiritual eyes and senses; this knowledge released to me by God who was just too big for my natural senses to grasp. I realized He was awakening me to a greater knowledge of Him. When His presence lifted, I ran into the office, fell into my purple chair, and cried out for Him as I had done every day for the previous six months since becoming a Christian. "OK Lord, I give You all of my life. I will serve You all my days. I freely give to You all I have." That was the moment when I surrendered to the call of God on my life.

My office building filled with the Lord's tangible glory. I became aware of a stirring in my spirit, and realized He'd released something deep that was to take me to a new level in Him. He had released an awareness of the knowledge of the Lord—a supernatural knowledge of just how big He really is.

When we operate in the Spirit of knowledge, we come to know God and maintain a deep communion with Him.

I had been spending every day in prayer and in the Word in pursuit of the knowledge of the Lord. I was so hungry. Even though I'd only been saved for a short while, I quizzed everyone, and practically begged for information about the Lord. I checked out every book from the local library on Christianity. I asked my brother, Leo Miller, who is an Assembly of God pastor, to send me everything he had that pertained to the Lord. The deeper I dug, the more I yearned for Him; the more I knew, the more I wanted; and the more I wanted, the more He filled me.

SPIRIT OF KNOWLEDGE DEFINED

I love the Spirit of knowledge. One of the functions of this aspect of the seven Spirits of God is an ability to *know God like you've never known Him before*. It is also an ability to *see from His perspective*. It is a view of the Holy Spirit that many don't have. I believe, though, that God is releasing the ability to know Him, above and well beyond anything we read, learn, or hear about Him in the natural. Isn't that what we want?

> *That Christ may dwell in your hearts through faith;*
> *that you, being rooted and grounded in love, may be*
> *able to comprehend with all the saints what is the*
> *width and length and depth and height—to know the*

love of Christ which passes knowledge; that you may be filled with all the fullness of God (Ephesians 3:17-19).

Have you ever been around somebody who is talking about the things of God, and it just totally grips your heart? You think that guy knows God. Those who know God intimately and in the fuller state of knowledge are like a magnet to those who yearn to know Him. They radiate His glory in their awareness and knowledge of Him. These people diffuse something that provokes you into saying, "I want to know God like that!" When you talk to them for even 15 minutes, you receive so much, because they speak to you from the *knowledge* of the flow of God.

Moses went up on the mountain to declare to the Lord, "I want to know You!" When he left the mountain his face radiated God's glory. People followed and trusted Moses because of his knowledge and intimacy with God.

PERCEIVING TRUTH

The Spirit of knowledge enables us to know God and brings us His ability to perceive, discern, and know truth without effort. Godly knowledge comes through revelation and not just through books. The very essence of the word *knowledge* is to be deeply acquainted with Him. You don't become deeply acquainted through just studying about Him.

There is a big difference between knowing *about* someone and actually knowing that person. We can all say we know a certain celebrity. But few can say they know them well enough to hang out with them. The principle is the same as you begin to flow in the realm of the Spirit of knowledge. We begin to move into the cleft of the rock, instead of just around the rock. It is a desire similar to that of the lover: "*O my dove, in the clefts of the rock, in the secret places of the cliff, let me see your face, let me hear your voice; for your voice is sweet, and your face is lovely"* (Song of Sol. 2:14). It is a divine knowledge—a supernatural ability to know Him as He reveals Himself to you. As we meet with Him, the Spirit of knowledge imparts divine revelation of the deep things of God.

With this knowledge we can see from God's perspective on a day-to-day basis. Here is the place that we begin to know Him and His ways. It is a place of deep calling to deep and actually receiving the deep things of God. As the Spirit of knowledge flows like a mighty river through your life, it will powerfully, profoundly, and forever change you. You will be diving into the depth of God's vastness, but also in the river of knowledge of the Lord. As the Lord flows out of your life, you will find others beginning to ask you about God. That's the Spirit of the Lord in action!

THE WHOOSH OF GOD

At a meeting where I was speaking, during the worship time a deep holiness came into the room. I was standing at the pulpit reading Revelation 4:8: *"Holy, holy, holy, Lord God Almighty, who was and is and is to come."* The Lord's holy presence literally invaded the santuary—as if the floodgates of a mighty dam had opened, and the river engulfed the room. The air became instantly electrified, and His presence fell in the whole sanctuary. I call it the *Whoosh of God.* That is exactly what it sounds and feels like.

As this whoosh came, I heard, *"kaloop, kaloop, plunk, kaloop."* The members of the worship team began falling one by one—sobbing before the Lord. The last person standing was my friend Dennis. At the keyboard, he was trying his best to keep playing, but the presence of God was just too much for him. *Kaloop*. He fell too.

I turned toward the audience. Many were weeping. Many were out on the floor under the power; others were bowed deeply, while others lay prostrate on the floor before the Lord. I was the only one standing. I got down quickly!

The atmosphere was filled with the knowledge of the Lord: His vastness, His tangible presence. Hundreds had a face-to-face encounter with the living God. God wrecked and radically transformed them as revival broke out.

The same type of thing took place in a small Texas town just a few months after I was saved. It seemed I lived in a realm of constant encounters with the Lord that launched me into many of the things that I am walking in today. I was asked to share at the youth meeting at our local church on a Wednesday night. In preparation on Wednesday afternoon, I opened the Bible to Acts chapter 2, and read the incredible story of how the Holy Spirit came like a rushing wind. So for several hours I prayed one distinct prayer: "Lord, come tonight like a mighty rushing wind. You did it then and You can come again that way tonight."

The kids of the small Texas town found out that the Miller boys' dad was going to be sharing, so many came out of curiosity to hear what I had to say.

That night I was so scared. I will never forget that moment in history as long as I live. I was standing in front of kids from the seventh grade up. I had no idea what was going to happen or what I was going to say. As I opened my mouth to share, the whole atmosphere of the room changed. *Whoosh!* I knew something was about to happen.

One of the kids came toward me. Was he angry at me? I didn't know. As he got closer, he literally lunged toward me. When his head hit my shoulder, he began to weep uncontrollably.

"I want what you have…I want to know God like you do!" he wept. At that moment we both fell to the ground weeping.

A few minutes later I remembered I was suppose to be the speaker, so I stood to my feet. I saw 33 kids standing there, also weeping, desiring to know God. The events of that night started a revival outbreak in that small Texas community. The Spirit of the knowledge of the Lord came into the gym, and people had a face-to-face encounter with the reality of the living God!

That's the realm of God we can and should look forward to. I believe that we are going to have meetings where God comes in such a capacity, such holiness, that people are going to cry out, "What must I do to be saved?" even before the altar call.

When we lift up our hands and declare that the place be filled with His presence, then *Whoosh!* God is so good, it's happened in many meetings! I have had many dreams and open visions of meetings like these and I know they will increase.

LIVING AS AN OVERCOMER

When the Spirit of knowledge is released to the Church, His precepts and His perspective are revealed. We begin to see as He sees, hear as He hears, and think as He thinks. We come into the mind and the heart of Christ. We begin to live daily as overcomers in the Spirit. In John 17:15 Jesus said He didn't want His followers to be taken out of the world. No! He said, "Let them stay here, because they can rejoice. Because I have overcome, they can overcome too."

The Lord in this hour wants to raise up a people who live day by day—not just every once in a while, not just in meetings every two weeks—as overcomers. Do you want to live that way? You can. "*These things I have spoken to you, that in Me you may* *have peace. In the world you will have **tribulation**; but be of good cheer, I have overcome the world"* (John 16:33).

HOLY MAGNIFICATION

The Holy Spirit magnifies God! When the Spirit of knowledge is released, it enlarges your ability to comprehend the vastness of God. Are you yearning for transformation? Allow the Holy Spirit to magnify God for you! Nothing is too great for God! *"The people who know their God shall be strong, and carry out great exploits"* (Dan. 11:32).

Right now the Spirit of knowledge is being released on the Body of Christ. Ask the Holy Spirit to come and rest upon you. Eagerly seek to know Him like you've never known Him before. He will answer. I believe that when this release of the Spirit of knowledge comes, the Church will be transformed from glory to glory to glory, and we will declare in one accord, "Behold Him!"

The apostle Peter, who operated in the Spirit of knowledge, wrote

> *Grace and peace be multiplied to you in the knowledge of God and of Jesus our Lord as His divine power has given to us all things* [I love the word *all*] *that pertain to life and godliness, through the knowledge of Him who called us by glory and virtue, by which had been given to us exceedingly great* [The Lord is always doing above and beyond.] *and precious promises, that through these you may be partakers of the divine nature* (2 Peter 1:2-4a).

It's your experiences in your Christian walk that bring you into a union with Christ, His stature and His nature. Words alone don't bring you into that union; it's He who lives in you who brings you there. There's nothing wrong with confessing the Scriptures until they becomes a light—a morning star in your heart. Remember to seek the knowledge of Him, so you can do all through Christ who strengthens you.

A MANTLE OF KNOWLEDGE

The Spirit of knowledge will release the fear of the Lord. How would you like to have a mantle of the knowledge of the Lord? Have you ever been around somebody who knows God and operates in that mantle?

I believe that men like Charles Finney functioned out of a mantle of the knowledge and the fear of the Lord. Such people could walk into a place, and without their saying a word, something was released that brought people into an encounter with God. The result was the salvation of many.

If you have ever watched Billy Graham on television, or attended one of his meetings, you know that his message is simple but powerful—salvation. There is always a great response.

A friend of mine—an established Christian of 25 years, a worship leader, and basically a very solid guy—related what he saw at a Billy Graham meeting. He said that as soon as Billy got behind the pulpit, something hit the whole coliseum. When Mr. Graham gave the altar call, my friend wanted to go down and get saved again, because something had hit the whole place! It was the knowledge of the Lord. Just imagine the Spirit of knowledge hitting an entire city!

I believe Jonathan Edwards had a mantle of knowledge and fear of the Lord. It has been said that Jonathan Edwards wore little wire-rimmed glasses and lacked charisma. But his preaching caused people to fall out of their seats, shake, and scream to get saved. His famous sermon, "Sinners in the Hands of an Angry God," sparked one of the "Great Awakening" revivals that began in New England. If you have you read this sermon, you may have thought, *I don't see how this caused an awakening*. But I believe that Edwards operated out of a mantle of the knowledge of God that released the fear of the Lord. They are partners together.

We should be like Moses on the mountain. "Lord, I don't want to go anywhere or do anything without You. I want to know You like I've never known You before. I want to become more deeply and intimately acquainted with You." In Exodus 33:13 (AMP) we read,

> *Now therefore, I pray You, if I have found favor in Your sight, show me now Your way, that I may know You [progressively become more deeply and intimately acquainted with You, perceiving and recognizing and understanding more strongly and clearly] and that I may find favor in Your sight. And [Lord, do] consider that this nation is Your people.*

PARTNERING WITH GOD

Jesus was sensitive to the Holy Spirit, and partnered with Him to do the Father's business even from a young age. When Mary and Joseph left 12-year-old Jesus behind in Jerusalem, and then returned to find Him, He asked, *"Why did you seek Me? Did you not know that I must be about My Father's business?"* (Luke 2:49)

Later when He reproved the Jews He said, *"My Father has been working until now, and I have been working"* (John 5:17).

That word *working* literally means "being about business." So Jesus essentially said, "My Father is about His business, and I'm simply *partnering with Him.*" Jesus affirmed that He was doing exactly what God was doing.

"Then Jesus answered and said to them, 'Most assuredly, I say to you, the Son can do nothing of Himself" (John 5:19a). Can you believe Jesus is saying this? If Jesus says this, how much more should we say it? *"But what He sees the Father do; for whatever He does, the Son also does in like manner. For the Father loves the Son, and shows Him all things that He Himself does; and He will show Him greater works than these, that you may marvel"* (John 5:19b-20).

What does Jesus mean by, "I see what My Father is doing, and then I do it?" It's spiritual perception, with which the Spirit of knowledge provides us, so that we can perceive truth.

Since He has called us to Him, we have been invited also to live life out of the powerful flow of the Spirit of knowledge, so that we may know Him and His ways. We are not just called to know the acts of God, but the God of the Acts! The flow of the Spirit of knowledge is supernatural ability from the Holy Spirit to know the things and secrets of God.

Do you hear the Spirit's heart? Pursue Him. Partner with Him. Pray to know Him, so that you may recognize and understand Him. Pray to live in that cleft of knowing Him. Pray for the *whoosh* of God.

Paul pursued after the living God. He hungered for Him:

> *Yes, furthermore, I count everything as loss compared to the possession of the priceless privilege (the overwhelming preciousness, the surpassing worth, and supreme advantage) of knowing Christ Jesus my Lord and of progressively becoming more deeply and intimately acquainted with Him [of perceiving and*

recognizing and understanding Him more fully and clearly]. For His sake I have lost everything and consider it all to be mere rubbish (refuse, dregs), in order that I may win (gain) Christ (the Anointed One). And that I may [actually] be found and known as in Him, not having any [self-achieved] righteousness that can be called my own, based on my obedience to the Law's demands (ritualistic uprightness and supposed right standing with God thus acquired), but possessing that [genuine righteousness] with comes through faith in Christ (the Anointed One), the [truly] right standing with God, which comes from God by [saving] faith. [For my determined purpose is] that I may know Him [that I may progressively become more deeply and intimately acquainted with Him, perceiving and recognizing and understanding the wonders of His Person more strongly and more clearly], and that I may in that same way come to know that power outflowing from His resurrection [which it exerts over believers], and that I may so share His sufferings as to be continually transformed [in spirit into His likeness even] to His death, [in the hope] (Philippians 3:8-10 AMP).

Wow! What an incredible heart after the Lord. "I count everything else as refuse compared to this one thing—to knowing You." This is the fullness found in the knowledge of Him.

REVELATION OF JESUS CHRIST

Paul shared that the knowledge he received did not come from flesh or blood but from the revelation of Jesus Christ:

For I want you to know, brethren, that the Gospel which was proclaimed and made known by me is not man's gospel [a human invention, according to or patterned after any human standard]. For indeed I did not receive it from man, nor was I taught it, but [it came to me] through a [direct] revelation [given] by Jesus Christ (the Messiah). You have heard of my earlier career and former manner of life in the Jewish religion (Judaism), how I persecuted and abused the church of God furiously and extensively, and [with fanatical zeal did my best] to make havoc of it and destroy it. And [you have heard how] I outstripped many of the men of my own generation among the people of my race in [my advancement in study and observance of the laws of] Judaism, so extremely enthusiastic and zealous I was for the traditions of my ancestors. But when He, Who had chosen and set me apart [even] before I was born and had called me by His grace (His undeserved favor and blessing), saw fit and was pleased [Isa. 49:1, Jer. 1:5] To reveal (unveil, disclose) His Son within me so that I might proclaim Him among the Gentiles (the non-Jewish world) as the glad tidings (Gospel), immediately I did not confer with flesh and blood [did not consult or counsel with any grail human being or communicate with anyone] (Galatians 1:11-16 AMP).

Since this was Paul's experience, he prayed by the inspiration of the Holy Spirit for every believer to know this great communion. *"That the God of our Lord Jesus Christ, the Father of glory, may give to you the spirit of wisdom and revelation in the knowledge of Him"* (Eph. 1:17). Also, *"For this reason we also, since the day we heard it, do not cease to pray for you, and to ask that you may be filled with the knowledge of His will in all wisdom and spiritual understanding"* (Col. 1:9).

GRACE AND PEACE

"*Grace and Peace be multiplied to you in the knowledge of God and of Jesus our Lord*" (2 Pet. 1:2). Head knowledge puffs up, but the Spirit of knowledge releases grace that will release the fruit of humility. All of Him and none of me. It forms a union of Spirit to spirit, heart to heart, deep to deep. We actually become partakes of His divine nature, to a place of divine union in the inner man. This is the place we are receiving pure knowledge of the Lord that will nurture us in the Word, and empower us to walk every day with a pure heart. We will grow in the stature of Christ, the hope of glory!

Remember the encounter that I had with the angel of the Lord? One of the names written on his arms was *Stature*. By His divine power we become partakers of His divine nature, the stature of Christ in us, but it can only happen in the knowledge of Him. I emphasize again that it is not head knowledge. It is what the Spirit of knowledge releases to bring us into that deep to deep embrace of the Spirit that wrecks us, transforms us, and imparts to us the mind of Christ.

The fullness of God and stature of Christ are exemplified so eloquently in this passage:

> That you may have the power and be strong to apprehend and grasp with all the saints[God's devoted people the experience of that love] what is the breadth and length, and height and depth of it]: [That you may really come] to know [practically, through experience for yourselves] the love of Christ, which far surpasses mere knowledge [without experience]: that you may be filled [through all your being] unto all the fullness of God [may have the richest measure of the divine

Presence, and become a body wholly filled and flooded with God Himself] (Ephesians 3:18-19 AMP).

The Holy Spirit wants us to see the weightier things of God, deeply rooted and ever expanding through the Spirit of knowledge. It is not by our ability to obtain this knowledge, rather, it is taught to us by the Revealer. He dives deep in the treasure chest of God's wisdom to reveal Himself to us, that our lives will be filled with His fullness.

This releases the demonstration of the Kingdom, not in words only, but in the demonstration and testimony of the Spirit. We are enabled to bring an awareness of knowledge of His presence to others. Our words will be supernatural ones from the floodgates of the overflow.

*H*oly Spirit, release a great river of the Spirit of knowledge in our lives, that we may know beyond anything we have ever known about You. With great joy we look forward to becoming partakers of Your divine nature. Let the lamp of the Spirit of knowledge burn deep within our hearts, creating in us a holy passion to hunger after You. Let our lives overflow with the fullness of God and bring many into the knowledge of His glory. "For the earth will be filled with the knowledge of the glory of the Lord as the waters cover the sea" (Hab. 2:14).

CHAPTER 15

The Spirit of the Fear of the Lord

"Let all the earth fear the Lord; let all the inhabitants of the world stand in awe of Him" (Psalm 33:8).

THIS expression of the sevenfold Spirits of God, the fear of the Lord, helps us desire to please and obey God in everything. We increase our capacity to know and experience Him in His glory. When we draw close in intimacy with the Father, we also receive the ability to see things from His perception or perspective.

AWE AND WONDER IN HIS PRESENCE

The fear of the Lord is awe and wonder in the presence of the Creator of the universe, the mighty, great, and awesome God—and the awareness of being in His presence every moment of every day. Mary praised God that His mercy extends to those who fear Him (see Luke 1:50). Paul called upon Christians to make holiness perfect in the fear of God (see 2 Cor. 7:1), to work out our salvation with fear and trembling (see Phil. 2:12), and to be subject to one another in the fear of Christ (see Eph. 5:21).

Even Peter told us to live our lives as strangers here in reverent fear (see 1 Pet. 1:17).

Reverence, love, trust, thankfulness, honor, and worship describe this fear. His attributes such as holiness, justice, power, and majesty inspire this reverence in us. The Bible tells us that His love, goodness, and forgiveness should inspire awe and worship in our hearts (see Ps. 67:7; 1 Sam. 12:24; Ps. 130:4). Jesus delighted in the fear of the Lord, as Isaiah prophesied describing Jesus in Isaiah 11:3. Shouldn't Jesus' delight be ours?

I remember I felt that delight and reverent awe in a powerful way and for the first time. We were in our second month of revival in the "War Zone" area of Albuquerque, New Mexico. I spent many hours in fasting and prayer, and we saw tremendous things happen every day. I was preparing for the service on the last day of the meetings, really pressing in for the heart of the Lord. On my knees in prayer with my head bowed low to the ground, I had a visitation from the Lord. (Now I had always thought that if I had the chance, I would ask Him about everything I wanted. I would tell Him how awesome He is. I couldn't wait.)

Well, in this instance, He didn't just casually walked into the room. It was boom, and He was there. The atmosphere changed instantly. I felt His presence so close, I didn't dare lift my head to look, but the Lord said, "Look!"

I said, "I can't, Lord. I'm going to die!" I really felt that! I thought, *This is it; He's come to get me!*

"Keith, look at Me!"

As I raised my head, my breath left me. I started hyperventilating. I thought I was dying. The glory and holiness were more than I could handle. I immediately bowed my head again, overcome by His presence. I was undone! I could completely relate to the apostle John's experience:

Then I turned to see the voice that spoke with me. And having turned I saw seven golden lampstands, and in the midst of the seven lampstands One like the Son of Man, clothed with a garment down to the feet and girded about the chest with a golden band. His head and hair were white like wool, as white as snow, and His eyes like a flame of fire; His feet were like fine brass, as if refined in a furnace, and His voice as the sound of many waters; He had in His right hand seven stars, out of His mouth went a sharp two-edged sword, and His countenance was like the sun shining in its strength. And when I saw Him, I fell at His feet as dead. But He laid His right hand on me, saying to me, " Do not be afraid; I am the First and the Last" (Revelation 1:12-17).

THE SOUND OF RUSHING WATERS

John described God's voice as the sound of many rushing waters, and I can relate. When God called my name it was like, "Keith, Keith, Keith, Keith, Keith," and it went deep, deep, deep, deep. Like sonic waves reverberating, *boom, deeper, boom, deeper, boom, deeper.* His voice was completely flooded with love and penetrated all the way to the deepest part of my soul. When He said "Keith," I knew deep inside that He was calling forth who He had created me to be. Unbelievable depths of love penetrated every area of my being. I received a fiery impartation of His passion deep in me—so deep that it's still like fire in my bones! I can't explain the depth of the love and deep admiration and reverence I received for Him. All I could do was praise Him, as the voice from the throne that said, *"Praise our God, all you His servants, those who fear Him, both small and great!"* (Rev. 19:5).

Later, when I could get up, and talk, I called my wife right away. Janet and I have been married for 28 years, and whenever something new happens I share it with her.

"Babe, you know how I love you so much?"

"Yes," she said.

I wept and wept and then said, "I love you even more."

GODLY FEAR AND DEEP LOVE

That realm of visitation took me to a completely new level spiritually, and brought our ministry to a new level, but it did much more than that. It blew the lid off my limited understanding of the width, the depth, and the height of God's love. It humbled me before Him. "*The fear of the Lord teaches a man wisdom, and humility comes before honor*" (Prov. 15:33 NIV).

My perspective changed in the way I ministered, and godly fear and deep love toward Jesus enveloped me. I wanted to be a finisher and fulfiller of that which He had given me. My delight was to do His will. I *knew* His love. I felt that Paul's prayer had come to pass for me personally:

> *That He would grant you, according to the riches of His glory, to be strengthened with might through His Spirit in the inner man, that Christ may dwell in your hearts through faith; that you, being rooted and grounded in love, may be able to comprehend with all the saints what is the width and length and depth and height— to know the love of Christ which passes knowledge; that you may be filled with all the fullness of God* (Ephesians 3:16-19).

I am convinced that one of the realms God loves to move in, particularly in visitation, is the realm of love. Our faith expands dramatically in the reality of the knowledge of the vastness of His love toward us.

SEEK HIS DEPTHS

Holy fear grows and increasingly flows through us, the more deeply we come to know Him. Walking in this knowledge and fear is not burdensome; it is freedom. As the One who created all things, the One who controls all things, the One who knows all things, He is worthy of great awe and honor. He is the beginning and end. *"The Lord Almighty is the one you are to regard as holy, He is the one you are to fear, He is the one you are to dread"* (Isa. 8:13 NIV).

When God spoke my name in Albuquerque, He had me in a healthy realm of the fear of the Lord. True fear of Him is a deep, deep realm of intimacy. It is also a realm of realizing He is glorious and holy. Can you imagine that realm of the Holy Spirit— that knowledge of Him and the fear of the Lord—hitting a whole city? Can a city be saved in a day? *"I now realize how true it is that God does not show favoritism but accepts men from every nation who fear Him and do what is right"* (Acts 10:34-35 NIV).

"Who will not fear You, O Lord, and bring glory to Your name? For You alone are holy. All nations will come and worship before You, for Your righteous acts have been revealed" (Rev. 15:4 NIV).

God's people are those who live in the fear of the Lord (Acts 9:31). In America, Charles Finney (1792-1875) was considered the father of modern revivalism, with over 500,000 conversions resulting from his ministry. The fear of the Lord was definitely upon this great forerunner of mass evangelists like Billy Graham and Dwight L. Moody.

One day, Mr. Finney walked into an industrial company with no goal other than to be shown the business, when a woman sitting nearby looked up from her sewing and made a casual remark to him. When she sat back to her sewing, something powerful came over her, and she fell out of her chair, weeping uncontrollably. Then her friend, sitting beside her, fell out of her own chair and cried out, "Mercy, oh God, save us!" The factory shut down for seven days and nearly everyone became born again including the owner of the factory. (See *Power From on High* by Charles Finney.) It had to be the fear of the Lord upon Mr. Finney. *"Let all the earth fear the Lord; let all the people of the world revere Him"* (Ps. 33:8 NIV).

KNOWLEDGE AND WISDOM

The first step toward true knowledge and wisdom is having the fear of the Lord. Happy is the soul that has been awed by a view of God's majesty, who has had a vision of God's awesome greatness, His ineffable holiness, His perfect righteousness, His irresistible power, His sovereign grace. *"The fear of the Lord teaches a man wisdom, and humility comes before honor"* (Prov. 15:33 NIV).

When we walk in this function of the sevenfold Spirit of God, we will serve the Lord in deep conviction of the soul to live a godly life and flee from everything that doesn't bring honor due His holy name.

Then the churches throughout all Judea, Galilee, and Samaria had peace and were edified [built up]. *And walking in the fear of the Lord and in the comfort of the Holy Spirit, they were multiplied* (Acts 9:31).

Oh fear the Lord, you His saints! There is no want [no lack] *to those who fear Him* (Psalm 34:9).

To this man will I look, even to him that is poor and of a contrite spirit, and trembleth at My word (Isaiah 66:2b KJV).

As high as the heaven is above the earth, so great is His mercy toward them that fear Him…Like as a father pitieth [has compassion on] *his children, so the Lord pitieth* [has compassion on] *them that fear Him* (Psalm 103:11,13 KJV).

DESIRE TO PLEASE THE LORD

The fear of the Lord is the Spirit of holy reverence—a respect for the awesomeness and majesty of God. *"Therefore since we are receiving a kingdom that cannot be shaken, let us have grace, by which we may serve God acceptably with reverence and godly fear. For our God is a consuming fire"* (Heb. 12:28-29).

The fear of the Lord is a place where we must live—a place of wanting to please Him above all others in our lives.

"His delight is in the fear of the Lord, and He shall not judge by the sight of His eyes, nor decide by the hearing of His ears" (Isa. 11:3). This is a great description of what living in the Spirit of fear of the Lord looks like. Instead of looking with our own eyes, we see through the eyes of Jesus and listen through the ears

of Jesus. Throughout His life, Jesus Himself demonstrated this powerfully. He did only the things He saw His Father doing; He spoke only the things He heard the Father saying. He said that His food or sustenance was the joy of carrying out the purposes of His Father.

Jesus found delight in this deep place of communion with the Father. *"For the Father loves the Son, and shows Him all things that He Himself does; and He will show Him greater works than these, that you may marvel"* (John 5:20). He found His delight in the fear of the Lord! What a great place to live!

In Chapter 12, on the Spirit of counsel, we looked at post-resurrection fishing story that had a miraculous ending. Something similar had happened earlier in Jesus' ministry. Luke 5:1-10 tells how Jesus had claimed the use of Simon Peter's fishing boat as a temporary pulpit. When He finished speaking, He told Peter and his friends to get in the boat, row to the deep part of the lake, and let down their nets. After Peter pointed out to the Lord that they had fished all night without catching anything, they reluctantly obeyed Jesus.

The result was such a huge catch of fish that Peter shouted to his partner in another boat, "Come over here! We have so many fish we can't handle them all!" They divided the catch between two boats, but there were still so many that both boats were in danger of sinking!

At this, knowledge of Jesus' identity hit Peter hard, and he fell to his knees and cried, "Please leave, for I am a sinful man, O Lord."

The fear of the Lord gripped his heart as the knowledge of the Lord was released.

GLORIFY HIM

Reverence and awe and godly fear of the Lord glorifies Him. In the song of Moses and of the Lamb, we hear, "*Who will not fear You, O Lord, and bring glory to Your name? For You alone are holy*" (Rev. 15:4a NIV). For in proper fear of the Lord, there is obedience, and intimacy, worship, trust, sacrifice, and love.

Just as the Lamb knew, receiving deeper depths of the knowledge of the Lord releases greater depths of delight in doing the will of the Father. It's a holy fear of God that is always strong within us, if we love Him. The more we love Him, the more time we will spend with Him, the more we will know Him, and the greater will be the godly fear of Him in our hearts. That holy fear will guide us in paths of wisdom, protecting us from entangling ourselves in things that are displeasing to the heart of God. "*And he said to man, 'The fear of the Lord—that is wisdom, and to shun evil is understanding'*" (Job 28:28 NIV).

DO NOT BE AFRAID

I believe we are about to see the fear of the Lord impact the world in a mind-blowing way. God is going to call His Church out, into the marketplace, and the world will not be able to deny His power.

Acts 2:43 relates that just after the move of the Holy Spirit on Pentecost, there were signs, wonders, and healings, and great fear gripped the city. The citizens didn't dare speak against the Church, because there was an obvious godly anointing on each one of her members. The people could not deny His power.

In the realms of visitation that we are about to experience, we will be just like John. Jesus had to say, "Do not be afraid. Fear not." Do you remember when Daniel had his visitation? The Bible says he fell down on his hands and knees and trembled. The word tremble means "to shake vigorously." That is the fear of the Lord. The angel of the Lord had to say to Daniel, "Do not be afraid." We will be in fear in these latter days, but not in shock.

BECOME AWESTRUCK

I reverence God, in part, because of what has happened to me. Would you like the realm of the fear of God to be released in your heart in such a capacity that you are overwhelmed and awestruck? I believe that's the same realm of God's presence that was released in the ministries of the great evangelists and revivalists of the past. People will cry out, "Lord, Lord, have mercy on us!"

Ask the Lord to open up Heaven and let a mighty outpouring of the Spirit of the knowledge of the Lord be released over your home, family, neighborhood, community, and city. Pray for faith for your city, your unsaved family, and co-workers to fall to their knees with the fear of the Lord upon them, crying out, "What, Lord, what must I do to be saved?" Hallelujah! Cities—entire cities in a day, I'm believing for that!

THE LAW THAT PRODUCES THE FEAR OF THE LORD

In the Old Testament, King David rejoiced in the law that produces the fear of the Lord (see Ps. 19). When God teams up knowledge with the reverent fear of the Lord and releases them, it's going to wreck lives. Rejoice in the law that produces the fear of the Lord. *"The eye of the Lord is on those who fear Him, on those who hope in His mercy"* (Ps. 33:18). Fear God, embrace knowledge, and touch lives for the Kingdom. *"Oh, give thanks to the Lord, for He is good! For His Mercy endures forever"* (1 Chron. 16:34).

CHAPTER 16

Seven Spirits Rejoice

HAVE you asked God how your life could help His Kingdom come on earth? When we first begin our spiritual journey, we are taught that only few receive a calling to do God's "greater works." If we are not one of those called, then we are free to choose any path, as long as we pursue spiritual growth. No one tells us that one day, we'll come to that proverbial fork in the road where we can no longer grow spiritually unless we give God our whole lives.

THY KINGDOM COME

God's Kingdom encompasses everything under His rule and reign, including everything here in this world. Believers live in His Kingdom and must view things from a Kingdom perspective. Jesus prayed, "*Your kingdom come. Your will be done on earth as it is in heaven*" (Matt. 6:10).

For God's Kingdom to come, it has to grow; and those not already in His Kingdom are invited to come in. When we enter into His Kingdom, we find nurture and healing, and our spiritual and physical needs are met. Love conquers hate, and good conquers evil.

We believers then, as active members in God's Kingdom, have a specific role in achieving Kingdom growth—this is our destiny in Him.

As we grow in the things of the Lord, pursue Him, and pursue our destiny, revelation becomes deeper, broader, and clearer; it's progressive. First Corinthians 13 says we see only in part. The Holy Spirit constantly teaches about the deep things of God, the mysteries of the Kingdom, to those who hunger after it. The Lord intends His Church, His sons and daughters, to walk in fullness. This means becoming a partaker with Jesus of the things God has released and made available to every citizen of His Kingdom.

Jesus said that His Father was always at work, and that His job was to do the work of the Father. He said that His food was to do God's will. God wants His concern to be ours too. Throughout God's Word, it is clear that we are to partake of those things He releases to us, to do His work. Jesus told us to seek first the Kingdom of God and all of our needs would be met.

Our role as overcomers and fulfillers of our divine destiny (the work of the Father) must consume us and become the reason we exist. Jesus staked a claim on our entire life, yet many of us withhold most of our life for ourselves.

We must yearn, therefore, to know Him as we've never known Him before. We must draw close to Him to learn the deep unto deep things of God.

GOD'S GOALS FOR US

There are three goals God has for our spiritual life. The first is intimate fellowship with Him. Jesus has to be our first love, our first priority, our Lord and our best friend. (See First Corinthians 1:9; Proverbs 21:21; Revelation 2:1-4; John 15:4-15.)

The second is to be completely one with Him. This is a desire to want and to submit to His will, His plans, His timing, and His priorities. We discover these things through intimacy with Him.

The third is to become more like Jesus—to grow in His character, His holiness, His purity, His love and devotion for God, His love and devotion for people, His peace, joy, patience, perseverance, kindness, goodness, gentleness, faithfulness, trust, and self control. Paul said, in Philippians 3:8, that he considered everything a loss compared to the surpassing greatness of knowing Christ Jesus as his Lord, for whose sake he lost all things.

INTIMACY

God places a desire and a passion in our hearts to do the things He calls us to do, *"For it is God who works in you to will and to act according to His good purpose"* (Phil. 2:13 NIV). We are the happiest and most joyful when we are in the middle of God's will and plan. We need to prayerfully seek God and ask Him to help us discern His special plan for us. He'll give us the blueprints; and the fullness of the Revealer, the Holy Spirit, will release His sevenfold blessings, to help us fulfill our destiny and carry out God's plan for our life.

God's presence and power will always be with us when He calls us. *"Set apart for me Barnabas and Saul for the work to which I have called them"* (Acts 13:2b NIV). The Greek word for *called* means that God "called them unto Himself" first to a love relationship with Him, and next to where His presence and His power would be at work. We only need to respond in faith and obedience—God will provide the power and the fullness of the Holy Spirit to get the job done. A great example of this is God's call to Moses to help lead His people out of Egypt, and how God provided everything Moses needed to fulfill His plan.

FIRE OF HIS LOVE

The greatest and deepest place of ministry comes from being rooted and grounded in the motivation of the love of Jesus that burns like fire in our bones. The most important reason for the outpouring of the Holy Spirit is so that we can comprehend and know His great love. (See Ephesians 3:16-21.) "*God is love*" (1 John 4:8b), so when we're filled with the fullness of His sevenfold Spirit we're overflowing with the fullness of His *love*.

The seven lamps of fire signify many things, but I'll highlight this: The lampstand in Heaven is supplied by pure oil so that the flames will burn. As long as there is a supply of fresh oil, the lamp will burn brightly. Jesus said we are the light of the world, the brilliancy of His glory that will shine brightly in the midst of the darkness. We have to daily tap into the fresh anointing of the Holy Spirit (see Ps. 92:10) to keep the seven flames burning.

When we minister out of this flow, we can't depend on yesterday's oil, or the flow will diminish, and we will no longer see the expressions of the sevenfold Holy Spirit through our lives. We must stay rooted in Him through the length, width, height, and breadth of that *love* so we will know the fullness of God. Then we will see the "above and beyond anything we can ask or think, but according to His mighty power so that Jesus gets all the glory and honor" (see Eph. 3:20, 21).

Jesus prayed, "Father, as We are one, let them also be one with Us" (see John 17:21). Love is the deepest and strongest place of ministry. It will no longer be we who live, but He who lives through us. We will no longer minister out of a measure or out of performance, because we will be fully yoked with Him. As He is, so are we!

BAPTISM OF FIRE

The Lord wants to release the baptism of fire to our temples. We are the temple of the Holy Spirit, and everything in our lives that is not silver and gold needs to be burned up (see 1 Cor. 3:12-17). The straw, stubble, and hay rob us of knowing His rest. When we enter His rest, we will be motivated by the leading and prompting of the Holy Spirit, not by human traditions and philosophies.

We need to ask for the fullness of the seven flames of fire to come upon us and burn away everything that keeps us from knowing the Anointed One and His anointing. Remember, the number seven represents, perfect, completeness, fullness, and consummation.

We need to have the fiery presence of the Holy Spirit bring a *consummation*, which means "to bring to an end or to finish," to the things that keep us in knowing Him. Knowing Him is much more than just knowing about Him, it is a place of *divine union*. We need to remove all hindrances so that we can say with Jesus, "It is finished."

"And from the throne proceeded lightnings, thunderings, and voices. Seven lamps of fire were burning before the throne, which are the seven Spirits of God" (Rev. 4:5). Ask for the baptism of fire and the flames of the seven Spirits of God to burn the hay, wood, stubble, and straw in your life. He'll purify and refine you:

> *"Behold, I send My messenger, and He will prepare the way before Me. And the Lord, whom you seek, will suddenly come to His temple, even the Messenger of the covenant [the Holy Spirit], in whom you delight. Behold, He is coming," says the Lord of hosts. "But who can endure the day of His coming? And who can stand*

when He appears? For He is like a refiner's fire and like launderers' soap. He will sit as a refiner and a purifier of silver; He will purify the sons of Levi, and purge them as gold and silver, that they may offer to the Lord an offering in righteousness" (Malachi 3:1-3).

I indeed baptize you with water unto repentance, but He who is coming after me is mightier than I, whose sandals I am not worthy to carry. He will baptize you with the Holy Spirit and fire. His winnowing fan is in His hand, and He will thoroughly clean out His threshing floor, and gather His wheat into the barn; but He will burn up the chaff with unquenchable fire (Matthew 3:11-12).

The Holy Spirit will burn up everything in our lives that is not gold and silver. Gold represents *divine nature*, and silver represents *redemption*.

He is releasing the fire to set God's people free from heavy burdens and uneasy yokes (see Matt.11:28-30). His prayer for us is John 17:21: *"That they all may be one, as You, Father, are in Me, and I in You; that they also may be one in Us, that the world may believe that You sent Me."*

PUT ON CHRIST

One day in a vision, I saw the Lord upon the throne, and He was looking to and fro all through the earth. Someone would get His attention, and the Lord would smile. It brought pleasure to Him to see these people. As He smiled, He reached back, tore off a piece of the mantle, dropped oil on the torn piece, and released it. I saw hundreds of mantles released this way. They alighted on people, they rested upon them, but then absorbed right into the person. That person then became an expression of that facet of Christ upon the earth. They didn't have the mantle on them; they *became* the expression of the mantle.

Several months ago, I had another similar prophetic encounter when I saw in a vision the Lord standing with the most beautiful mantle I have ever seen. It was so alive, like flowing water. The essence of the beauty of the mantle was not the color or such, but how living and refreshing the mantle looked. It is almost impossible to put into words. The closest I can come to describing it is that it looked like living water in the form of a cloth that draped across the Lord's outstretched arms. The Lord said, "I am loosing my people. They will become who they are." The encounter was over. As I prayed about this encounter, the Holy Spirit began showing me the meaning of the vision.

> *Beware lest anyone cheat you through philosophy and empty deceit, according to the tradition of men, according to the basic principles of the world, and not according to Christ. For in Him dwells all the fullness of the Godhead bodily; and you are complete in Him, who is the head of all principality and power (Colossians 2:8-10).*

Paul uses strong language here by the leading of the Holy Spirit to get our attention. "Beware lest anyone cheat you." *Cheat* means "to plunder or to take captive." Wow! Paul says here that we can be plundered and in captivity because of traditions, philosophy, empty deceit, and the principles of this world.

The mantle that I saw in the encounter is Jesus' mantle. We need to put on Christ. We have been set free from bondage, but we are not fully enjoying all that we have received the moment He gave us the victory. Galatians 5:1 says, "*Stand fast therefore in the liberty by which Christ has made us free, and do not be entangled again with a yoke of bondage."* Jesus says, *"Come to Me, all you who labor and are heavy laden, and I will give you rest.* [Rest means "to be released from your toil or labor.] *Take My yoke upon you and learn from Me, for I am gentle and lowly in heart, and you will find rest for your souls. For My yoke is easy* [easy means "useful, pleasant, good, suitable, and serviceable"] *and My burden is light"* (Matt. 11:28-30).

That is the Lord's heart for you! His heart is that we be loosed from all that has taken us captive and plundered us from living life in the Anointed One and His anointing. He wants us to live in the fullness of all that He intends for us.

THE ZEAL OF THE LORD

The seven flames of fire also release the zeal of the Lord. We are to be *"not lagging in diligence, fervent in spirit, serving the Lord"* (Rom 12:11). *Fervent* means "living fervor, fiery hot, full of burning zeal." It is the opposite of dignified, cold, and unemotional. In a Christian context, it signifies a high spiritual temperature inflamed by the Holy Spirit. If we allow the oil to cease to flow in our lives, we will lose the zeal of the Lord! The zeal of the Lord is a baptism of His love, so that all we do will be out a deep love for Him. His passion burns in my bones like fire! The zeal of the Lord is not religious zeal or man's zeal; it is *His love.*

In this place, we bring forth the increase of the Kingdom. The fire burns up everything that causes us to labor in traditions and performance, and we become yoked with Him so that we are in rest (see Heb. 4:9); that is the greatest flow, Him through us.

Of the increase of His government and peace there will be no end, upon the throne of David and over His kingdom, to order it and establish it with judgment

and justice from that time forward, even forever. The
zeal of the Lord of hosts will perform this (Isaiah 9:7).

Do you see that as we are in this place of walking and living
in fresh oil, we are plugged in and become partakers of His
divine nature? (See Romans 11:16-17, Zechariah 4:11, Psalm
92:10.) We will see the sevenfold flow of the Holy Spirit, the
seven lamps of fire, and we will operate in the zeal of the Lord as
we partake of His fresh oil for our lives.

THE PLUMB LINE

Look again at one of my favorite passages, Zechariah 4:10b:
"These seven rejoice to see the plumb line in the hand of
Zerubbabel." The *plumb line* is a building tool: a piece of string
attached to a ball of lead, and it shows the builder if the walls
being built are straight and perpendicular to the foundation.
"These seven rejoice." The sevenfold Holy Spirit rejoices when
the Church executes the building and government of the
Kingdom of God (Zerubbabel represents government). The
Church will begin to function out of the full, sevenfold ministry
of the Holy Spirit, when it builds by the blueprint of Heaven, the
commissioning of the Lord. Even the world will begin to take
notice when this happens. (See John 17:23.)

Even now, God speaks this great word of encouragement to
the builders of your living temple; *"The hands of Zerubbabel*
have laid the foundation of this house; his hands shall also fin-
ish it; and thou shalt know that the Lord of hosts hath sent me
unto you. For who hath despised the day of small things?"
(Zech. 4:9-10a). Even though you may have a small beginning, do
not despise it, because you are going to be a finisher like
Zerubbabel.

Look at the result in Isaiah 11:3 of ministering out of this capacity. It says, *"His delight is in the fear of the Lord, and He shall not judge by the sight of His eyes, nor decide by the hearing of His ears."* Jesus lived in this dimension: *"I can of Myself do nothing. As I hear, I judge; and My judgment is righteous, because I do not seek My own will but the will of the Father who sent Me"* (John 5:30). He never did anything but what He heard and saw the Father doing. We are here to bring forth justice and righteousness. The Church is coming into her greatest hour, and we are going to see increase of the implementation of justice and righteousness upon the earth. But we have to be in a place where it is not by our ability that we implement justice and righteousness. Watch this:

> *He shall not judge by the sight of His eyes, nor decide by the hearing of His ears; but with righteousness He shall judge the poor, and decide with equity for the meek of the earth; He shall strike the earth with the rod of His mouth, and with the breath of His lips he shall slay the wicked. Righteousness shall be the belt of His loins, and faithfulness the belt of His waist* (Isaiah 11:4-5).

That is not just referencing poverty. It is about those who are poor in spirit. Jesus said that He came to preach good news to the poor (see Luke 4:18). That is the Word of the Lord.

JUDGMENT AND JUSTICE

This is why we need to function out of the sevenfold flow of the Holy Spirit. We need to live just as Jesus lived: He ministered out of divine union with the Father, knowing the heart and mind of the Father, and delighting in the fear of the Lord to do His Father's bidding only. He functioned out of the sev-enfold Holy Spirit, or the full ministry of the person of the Holy Spirit. He did not know measure. He ministered out of unlimit-ed anointing.

If you continue reading in Zechariah 4:11-14, you will see a generation that is going to minister out of the perpetual ceaseless supply of the fullness of the Holy Spirit, and they will have hands that drip with oil; they will be called "children of fresh oil."

We will build the things He has purposed for such a time as this by the sevenfold Spirit as wise master builders. We will order and establish with judgment and justice by the zeal of the Lord, His love that burns deep with us. All that we do we will do because of Him.

> *You have a mighty arm, strong is Your hand, and high is Your right hand. Righteousness and justice are the foundation of Your throne; mercy and truth go before Your face. Blessed are the people who know the joyful sound! They walk, O Lord in the light of Your countenance. In Your name they rejoice all day long, and in Your righteousness they are exalted. For You are the glory of their strength, and in Your favor our horn is exalted. For our shield belongs to the Lord, and our King to the Holy One of Israel* (Psalm 89:13-18).

We are called to bring forth godly judgment and justice upon the earth. As it is in Heaven, so will it will be upon the earth. We are to render a verdict against all unrighteousness, declare the vengeance of our God; and to see those who are bound, loosed, to see those who are in captivity, freed.

SUMMARY

Are you willing to give God your whole life? If your heart is devoted to Him and His work (your destiny), then He will unfold the deep and mysterious secrets of the Kingdom through wisdom and understanding, counsel and might, knowledge and the fear of the Lord. He'll give you those things and more through the fullness of the sevenfold Spirits of God. The Lord searches for those who desire to live in the flow of His unlimited anointing. Is that you? Cry out to Him, "Lord, do something in me that is way beyond me!" Ask Him for the impossible, the extraordinary, the shock and awe—so people will say, "I want what you have. How do I get it?" God will empower you to win whole cities for Him—if you'll let Him. He has the blueprints, and He's given us the Helper.

Reflections:
Surrendering to the Spirit

_____

_____

_____

_____

_____

_____

_____

_____

_____

_____

_____

For More Information

Keith Miller of Stand Firm World Ministries is a fiery man of God who moves powerfully in the prophetic, miracles, signs, wonders, and healings. Flowing with revelation and anointing, he releases the presence of the Holy Spirit and sparks revival fires everywhere he goes.

Keith's teaching is anointed and rock solid, imparting revelation and an unshakeable trust in the truth of God's promises. The words he preaches, the scriptures he unpacks, and the strongholds he pulls down, release those who sit under his ministry to new levels of boldness, faith, and the ability to stand firmly on the promises of God.

Holy Spirit downloads are as common in Keith's meetings as healings and miracles. The words of knowledge he moves in create an atmosphere of faith in believers that allows God to increase in their lives, homes, families, neighborhoods and regions. Through Keith's ministry, the Lord has empowered thousands of Christians throughout the US and abroad to help establish and advance the Kingdom of God by activating believers into the fullness of their God - Given Destiny and see breakthrough for breakout in every area of their lives.

For more information contact

STAND FIRM WORLD MINISTRIES

P. O. Box 51971, Amarillo, TX 79159

Phone: 1-806-468-7179

keith@sfwm.org

For more information about their conferences, schools, resources or more information about inviting Keith Miller to your city or region, visit their website or email them at:

www.sfwm.org

Bookings@sfwm.org

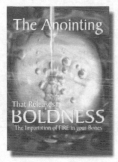

KEITH MILLER RESOURCES
FROM
STAND FIRM WORLD MINISTRIES

THE POWER OF IMPARTATION
Activation of Impartation

Teaching CD ~ by Keith Miller

Romans 1:11 "For I long to see you so that I may impart to you some spiritual gifts so that you may be established.

The Lord wants to give you a divine deposit to establish you. It's a divine deposit from the Throne Room to impart to you to keep you in destiny. To have eyes to see and ears to hear. A Divine Impartation of every good gift given to you by the Father. Activate the deposits of Impartation that God has placed in you for your destiny.

RIVERS OF OIL
Beyond The Measure

Teaching CD ~ by Keith Miller

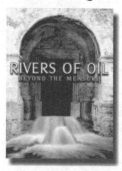

Just as God sent Jesus, who ministered out of an anointing without measure, God wants you to begin to minister and operate out of the ceaseless, perpetual flow of the Holy Spirit like rivers of oil flowing from the throne. God never intended for the Church to move in a limited measure of anointing. He always wanted us to have the fullness of the Holy Spirit. Now is the time to press in for everything that the Lord has for his children.

Additional copies of this book and other
book titles from DESTINY IMAGE are
available at your local bookstore.

Call toll free: 1-800-722-6774.

Send a request for a catalog to:

Destiny Image® Publishers, Inc.
P.O. Box 310
Shippensburg, PA 17257-0310

"Speaking to the Purposes of God for this
Generation and for the Generations to Come."

For a complete list of our titles,
visit us at www.destinyimage.com